TEACHER RE
FOR PRACTICE A
WITH ANSWER KEY

M c G R A W - H I L L

SCIENCE

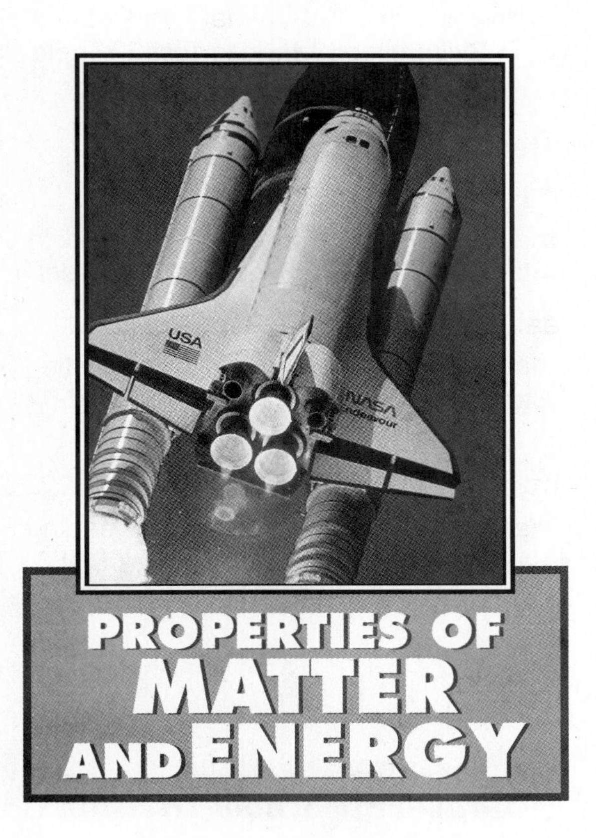

PROPERTIES OF MATTER AND ENERGY

McGraw-Hill School Division
New York Farmington

The TRPS Contains:	
Data Sheets for PE Activities (also in ***Science Journal***)	Explore Activities • Skill Builders • Quick Labs
Data Sheets for TE Activities (BLMs only)	Alternative Explore Activities
Reading Suppport (BLMs only)	Reading Study Guides • Study Aids • Summaries • Cloze Tests
Practice Worksheets (also in ***Science Practice Workbook***)	Topic Practices • Chapter Practices

Properties of Matter and Energy

Chapter: Properties and Changes

Chapter: Temperature, Heat, and Energy

McGraw-Hill School Division
A Division of The ***McGraw-Hill*** *Companies*

McGraw-Hill School Division
Two Penn Plaza
New York, New York 10121

Printed in the United States of America
ISBN 0-02-277652-4 / 6
3 4 5 6 7 8 9 047 04 03 02 01 00

Name ____________________

Investigate What Things Float on Others

Hypothesize How can the fact that a substance floats help you identify the substance? Why does one substance float over another?

Write a **Hypothesis:**

____

____

____

____

Identify substances by how they float on top of each other.

Materials

- 100-mL graduated cylinder
- blue food coloring
- small piece of cork
- balance and masses
- spoon
- small lump of clay
- small (birthday) candle
- goggles
- four 10-mL graduated cylinders (for measuring the liquid)
- 20 mL each of corn oil, baby oil, corn syrup, and water, each in a plastic cup

Procedures  **Safety** Wear goggles.

1. **Measure** Pour 20 mL of water into the 100-mL graduated cylinder, and add one drop of food coloring. Stir.
2. **Measure** Measure out 20 mL of corn oil into a plastic cup. Slowly pour the corn oil down the spoon into the water. Describe what happens.

   ____

3. **Experiment** Continue the process in step 2 by adding 20 mL each of the baby oil and then the corn syrup.

   ____

Conclude and Apply

1. **Compare and Contrast** What happened to the liquids as you added them to the cylinder?

2. Communicate In what order were the liquids arranged? On a separate piece of paper, draw and label an illustration that shows which liquids appeared on top, in the middle, and on the bottom.

____

____

Going Further: Problem Solving

3. Predict How will other objects float or sink in the water—a lump of clay, a birthday candle, a piece of cork? Make a prediction and test your ideas.

____

____

4. Experiment Why do the liquids stack up as they do? How might using equal amounts of the liquids and a balance help you tell?

____

____

____

____

____

Inquiry

Think of your own question related to density. Can a higher density material float on a lower density material?

My Question Is:

____

How I Can Test It:

____

____

My Results Are:

____

____

Thinking About Sinking

Materials

- balance
- paper towels
- large bowl of water
- similar-sized cubes of margarine, chocolate, bouillon, and sugar

Procedures

1. Observe the materials your teacher gives you. Compare the volumes of the cubes.
2. If a balance is available, find the mass of each cube. If you do not have a balance, estimate the mass, and rank the cubes from least mass (1) to most mass (4). Record your data in the table below.

Material	Mass	Behavior in Water
Margarine		
Chocolate		
Bouillon		
Sugar		

3. Place each of the cubes in a bowl of water and record what happens.

Conclude and Apply

1. How did the volumes of the four cubes compare?

____

2. Which cube seemed to have the most mass? Which had the least mass?

____

____

3. How does the mass of the objects affect what happens when you place them in water?

____

____

____

Physical Properties

In this topic you will learn about how the physical properties of matter can be described.

Any solid, liquid, or gas is called **matter.** Matter is the "stuff" that makes up the world. You can measure an object's mass by trying to push or pull it.

Mass is a measure of how hard it is to push or pull an object. The more mass an object has, the harder it is to push or pull. The amount of the pull of gravity between an object and Earth is called the object's weight. Objects with more mass also have more weight. The amount of space taken up by an object is called its **volume.** Scientists often measure volume of solids in cubic centimeters, or cm^3. A cubic centimeter is the volume of a cube that measures one centimeter on each side. A graduated cylinder is used to measure liquid volume. The unit shown on a graduated cylinder is a milliliter, or mL ($1\ mL = 1\ cm^3$). The amount of mass in a certain volume of material is its **density.** You can find the density of an object by finding the mass, finding the volume, and dividing the mass by the volume. When an object is placed in a less dense liquid or gas, the object will sink toward the bottom. If the liquid or gas is more dense, the object will float toward the top.

Objects can be described by their properties. Properties are things you can observe with your senses. Some properties include color, hardness, odor, and shine. A **physical property** is a property that can be observed without changing the identity of a substance. Properties such as color, odor, and density are physical properties. When a substance changes from solid to liquid or liquid to gas, it is changing its state. A **physical change** is a change of size, shape, or state without forming a new substance. Mixing things together is a type of physical change. A **solution** is a mixture of one substance dissolved in another so that the properties are the same throughout. There are many kinds of solutions. Solutions may contain any combination of solids, liquids, and gases.

A **chemical change** is a change in matter that produces new substances with properties different from the original substances. Chemical changes often show one or more key signs. A color change may occur, heat and light may be given off, a gas may be produced, or a powdery solid may form. The mass of matter does not change during chemical changes. The total mass of all starting substances equals the total mass of all new substances in chemical changes.

Pressure is the weight or force on a given area. All matter, including fluids, can exert some kind of presssure on any object. Fluids also push objects. Once objects are submerged in a fluid, the fluid exerts a buoyant force on the object. Due to this force, objects seem to lose weight when placed underwater.

Physical Properties

Fill in the blanks.

How Can You Measure Matter?

1. Any solid, liquid, or gas is ____________________.

2. The more ____________________ an object has, the harder it is to push or pull.

3. The amount of space taken up by an object is its ____________________.

What Things Float on Others?

4. The amount of mass in a given amount of space is the ____________________ of an object.

5. An object that is floating is ____________________ dense than the liquid or gas it is in.

How Else Can You Describe Matter?

6. Properties such as color and odor are ____________________ properties.

7. Physical properties can be observed without changing the ____________________ of the substance.

How Can Heat Help to Describe Matter?

8. A substance that changes from solid to liquid or liquid to gas, changes its ____________.

9. The temperature at which a substance changes from a solid to a liquid is called the ______________________________.

10. The temperature at which a substance changes from a liquid to a gas is called the ______________________________.

11. The particles of a substance will move faster if ____________________ is added to it.

12. When the particles of a substance move about faster, they spread out, causing the substance to ____________________.

How Can Things Change and Still Stay the Same?

13. Any change that does not produce new substances is a(n) ______________________________.

What Are Solids, Liquids, and Gases Like?

14. Something that has a definite shape and volume is called a(n) ______________.

15. Something that has a definite volume and takes the shape of its container is called a(n) ______________.

How Can Substances Be Mixed Together?

16. Any combination of two or more substances in which the substances keep their own properties is a(n) ______________.

17. A mixture made of parts that separate upon standing is a(n) ______________.

What Other Types of Mixtures Are There?

18. A mixture in which one substance dissolves in another so that the properties are the same throughout is a(n) ______________.

19. The part of a solution that dissolves a substance is called the ______________.

How Do Things Change Identity?

20. New substances are produced with physical properties different from the starting substances in a(n) ______________.

What Happens to Mass in Chemical Changes?

21. The total mass of all starting substances ______________ the total mass of all new substances in a chemical change.

22. When any object is submerged in a fluid, the fluid exerts ______________ ______________ on the object.

How Can We Use Buoyant Force?

23. If the weight of a submerged object is greater than the buoyant force acting on it, the object will ______________.

24. Decreasing your ______________ by taking a deep breath helps you float in water.

Physical Properties: Volume

Some diagrams illustrate cause-and-effect relationships. A cause-and-effect relationship shows how two different events are related. The first event to occur is the cause. It triggers a second event, or effect, to happen. Look at the diagram below. Think about the cause-and-effect relationship it shows. Then answer the questions.

When the rock is placed in the water, the water rises and pours out of the spout.

Here enough water pours out to fill four cubes that are 1 centimeter on a side. This means the rock has a volume of 4 cm^3.

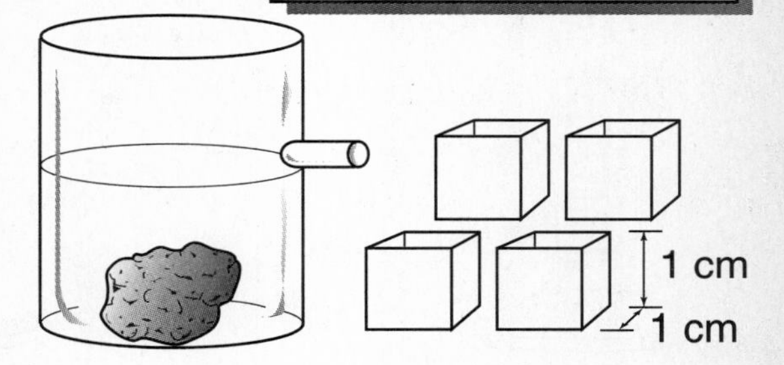

1. What does the arrow indicate?

____

2. What effect does this have on the water?

____

3. What do the four cubes represent?

____

____

4. What trait of the rock do the cubes show?

____

5. What is the volume of the rock? ______________

Name ______________________________

Physical Properties: States of Matter

Some diagrams illustrate changes that occur to substances. Look at the diagram below. Compare the parts of the diagram. Think about how they are alike and different. Then answer the questions.

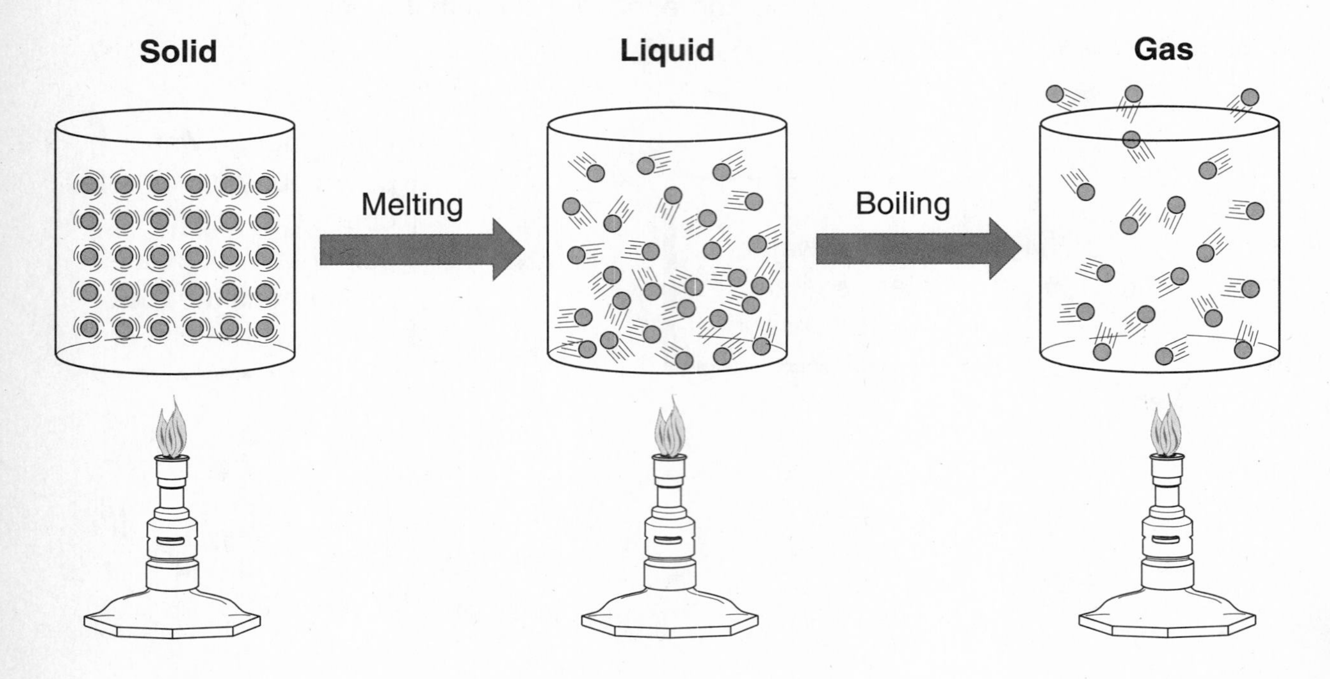

1. What do the spheres inside the beakers represent?

____

2. What changes occur when the substance is melted?

____

3. What changes occur when the liquid substance is boiled?

____

____

____

4. What similarities exist in the beaker in all three parts of the diagram?

____

____

5. What causes the changes shown in the diagram? ______________

Name ____________________

Catch the Gas!

Hypothesize Does total mass change in a chemical change?

Write a **Hypothesis:**

____

____

Materials

- magnesium ribbon
- narrow test tube
- small beaker
- goggles
- vinegar
- balance
- balloon

Procedures

Safety Wear goggles.

1. Half-fill a small test tube with vinegar. Place a thumb's-length piece of magnesium ribbon into the test tube. Stretch the balloon opening over the top of the test tube to form a cap.
2. **Measure** Stand up the test tube in a small beaker. Find the mass of the entire setup. Then observe for a while. Find the mass again. Record your results.

   ____

Conclude and Apply

1. **Observe** What signs did you observe that a chemical change occurred?

   ____

   ____

   ____

2. **Compare and Contrast** How did the mass of the starting materials compare to the mass of the materials after the chemical change? Is this what you expected? Explain.

   ____

   ____

Going Further How might changing the system affect the measurements of the mass? Write and conduct an experiment.

My Hypothesis Is:

____

____

My Experiment Is:

____

____

My Results Are:

____

____

____

Name ____

Physical Properties

Fill in the blanks.

In a mixture, two or more substances that keep their own ____________ are combined. You can use a(n) ____________ to separate an iron particle and sulfur mixture. In perfumes, substances are blended together to create pleasing ____________. However, some of the perfume substances by themselves might have foul ____________. Perfume ____________ can recognize individual scents. A mixture made of parts that separate upon standing is called a(n) ____________. In this mixture, solid particles separate by settling to the ____________, while fine particles float. Particles can be separated using a(n) ____________ or strainer. An example of a(n) ____________ is water and oil. These two ____________ do not mix together.

Physical Properties

Match the correct letter with the description.

_____ **1.** any solid, liquid, or gas

_____ **2.** a measure of how hard it is to push or pull an object

_____ **3.** the amount of space taken up by an object

_____ **4.** the amount of mass in a given amount of space

_____ **5.** properties that can be observed without changing the identity of a substance

_____ **6.** the temperature at which a substance changes from a solid to a liquid

_____ **7.** the temperature at which a substance changes from a liquid to a gas

_____ **8.** a combination of two or more substances in which the substances keep their own properties

_____ **9.** a mixture of one substance dissolved in another so that the properties are the same throughout

_____ **10.** a change in matter that produces a new substance with different properties from the original

a. mixture
b. mass
c. physical properties
d. volume
e. chemical change
f. melting point
g. density
h. solution
i. matter
j. boiling point

Answer each question.

11. What happens to an object when it is placed in a less dense liquid or gas?

____

12. Name three physical properties that can help identify a substance.

____

13. When swimming, how does taking in a deep breath help you float?

____

14. After a chemical change, which has a greater mass: the starting substances or the new substances?

____

Name ____

Design Your Own Experiment

What Is Inside the Mystery Box?

Hypothesize What if you were given a mystery box with things inside? How could you tell what was inside the box without looking inside it?

Write a **Hypothesis:**

____

____

Materials

- container, such as a shoe box
- various objects, such as paper clips, marbles, and coins
- paper towels or newspapers (optional)
- ruler
- magnet

Procedures

1. **Plan** (First lab partner) Make a mystery box out of the view of your lab partner. Put various materials in the container. You may line the container with paper towels or newspaper to make it more difficult for your partner to guess what's inside.

2. **Observe/Analyze** (Second lab partner) Observe the shape of the container you are given. Make any measurements you think might help you describe its contents. Note these measurements.

   ____

3. **Plan** (Second lab partner) Carefully tilt the box. Shake it. Hold the magnet next to the box, and run it back and forth across the surface. Make any observations you can. Write these observations.

   ____

   ____

4. **Experiment** Switch roles with your partner.

Conclude and Apply

1. **Hypothesize** Make a hypothesis about the inside structure or contents of the box. Does it have separate compartments? Record your hypothesis. On a separate piece of paper, draw what you think the inside of the box looks like.

____

____

2. **Analyze** How did you develop your hypothesis about the interior structure of the sealed box?

____

____

Going Further: Problem Solving

3. **Hypothesize** What else might you do to try to determine the contents of the sealed box?

____

____

Inquiry

Think of your own question related to indirect observations. What conclusions do scientists make based on indirect observations?

My Question Is:

____

____

How I Can Test It:

____

____

My Results Are:

____

____

____

What's Inside?

Materials

- wrapped "mystery present"
- magnet

Procedures

1. Your teacher will give your group an object that is wrapped in paper so that you cannot see what the object is.
2. With your group, discuss some way that you might investigate the object without opening the package and looking inside. List your ideas.

____

____

3. Use some of the group's ideas to investigate the object. Record the test and the results.

Test	Observation

4. If time permits, exchange "mystery presents" with another group and try to identify the new object.

Conclude and Apply

1. What do you think was in the package? Explain your answer.

____

____

2. Did the group with which you exchanged "mystery presents" come to the same conclusions your group did?

____

3. Your teacher will tell you what was in the package. Did you correctly identify the object? If not, what observation do you think misled you?

____

Elements and Atoms

In this topic you will learn about the atoms and elements that make up the matter we use.

There are at least 112 pure substances that cannot be broken down further into anything simpler. These substances are called **elements.** All matter in the world is made of elements. Elements can be solids, liquids, or gases.

Elements are made of very tiny particles called atoms. An **atom** is the smallest particle of an element that has the same chemical properties as the element. The atoms of one element are different from the atoms of any other element. Because each element is made of a particular type of atom, it has its own special properties. In 1803, John Dalton presented a simple atomic theory, concluding that gases were made up of solid particles with spaces between them.

An atom's dense center, where most of its mass is located is called a **nucleus.** The nucleus contains particles called protons and neutrons. A **proton** is a positively charged particle inside an atom's nucleus. A **neutron** is a particle with no charge inside an atom's nucleus. Both of these particles have about the same mass. The nucleus is held together by nuclear force.

An **electron** is a negatively charged particle that moves around an atom's nucleus. Electrons are about 1,800 times less massive than protons. They are held near the nucleus by electrical attraction to the protons. An atom has an equal number of protons and electrons, which makes the atom electrically neutral.

The atoms of each element have a unique number of protons. The number of protons in an atom is called its **atomic number.** The number of protons in an atom tells us what element it is.

Scientists have discovered about 112 different elements. These elements are arranged in increasing atomic number to form the Periodic Table of Elements. In 1868, Dmitry Mendeleyev arranged elements according to atomic mass, and discovered a repetitive pattern to several properties, including density, metal character, and ability to react with other elements. Any repeating pattern is called periodic. According to properties, elements can be placed into one of three groups: metals, metalloids, and nonmetals. **Metals** are any group of elements that conduct heat and electricity, are shiny when polished, and bend rather than break. Nonmetals are just the opposite. Metalloids have only some of the properties of metals. Each of these groups falls in a certain part of the periodic table.

Elements and Atoms

Fill in the blanks.

What Are the Simplest Substances?

1. All matter in the world is made of ____________.

2. Elements can be chemically combined to form ____________ like salt and sugar.

3. The smallest particle of an element that has the chemical properties of the element is a(n) ____________.

What Is Inside the Mystery Box?

4. For centuries, scientists have been trying to find out what is inside ____________.

5. The idea that tiny ____________ make up matter came from the Greek philosopher Democritus.

6. John Dalton said that gases were made up of solid particles with ____________ between them.

What Are Atoms Made Of?

7. The densest part of an atom is the ____________ where most the atom's mass is located.

8. A positively charged particle inside an atom's nucleus is a(n) ____________.

9. A particle with no charge inside an atom's nucleus is a(n) ____________.

10. A negatively charged particle that moves around an atom's nucleus is a(n) ____________.

How Have Ideas About Atoms Changed?

11. An element's ____________ is the number of protons in an atom of the element.

12. The mass of an atom is the total number of protons and ____________.

What Are Elements Like?

13. Mercury is one of the few elements that is a(n) ______________ at room temperature.

14. While compounds that contain ______________ are common, this substance is never found as an element in nature.

Are There Patterns in the Properties of Elements?

15. The Russian scientist ______________ discovered a repetitive pattern to several properties of the elements.

16. Mendeleyev's discovery is called the ______________________ of elements.

What Is the Modern Periodic Table Like?

17. In the modern form of the periodic table, elements are arranged in order of increasing ______________________.

18. According to their properties, elements can be placed in one of three groups—______________, metalloids, or nonmetals.

What Are Metals and Nonmetals?

19. As a group, metals ______________ electricity.

20. Most nonmetals are poor conductors of ______________ and electricity.

What Are Metalloids?

21. The properties of ______________ fall between the properties of metals and nonmetals.

22. The most abundant element in Earth's solid surface is ______________.

23. Steel is an example of a metallic mixture called a(n) ______________.

Elements and Atoms: Models of Atoms

A model is a representation of an object. Scientists use models to understand the structure of items in the natural world. Look carefully at the models below. Notice how the parts form the whole. Then answer the questions.

Models of helium and boron atoms

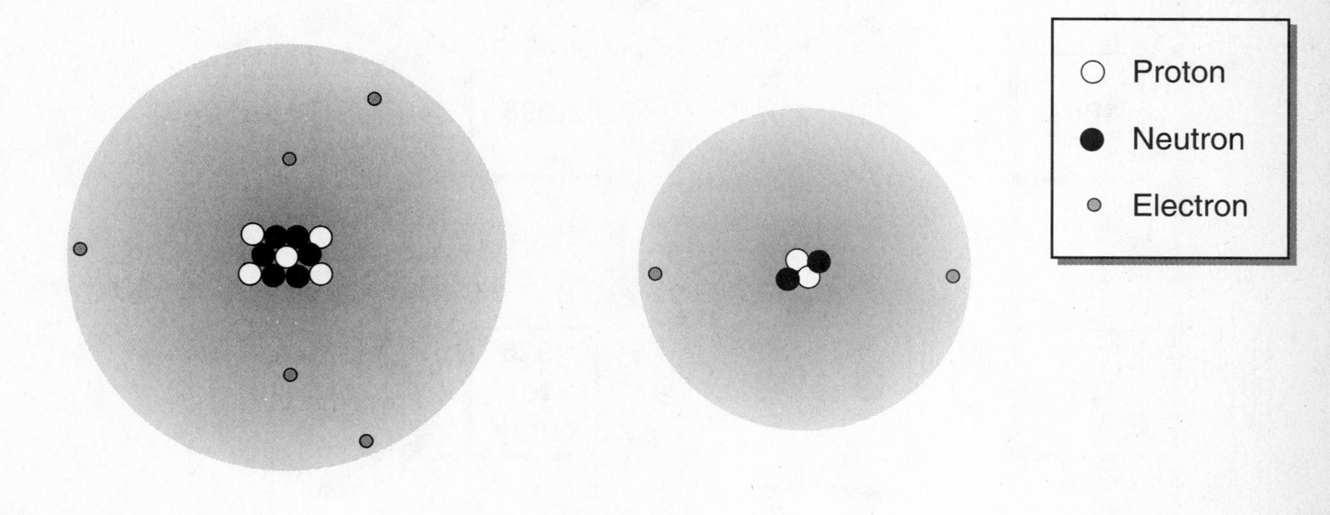

Boron **Helium**

1. What do the models represent?

____

2. What parts make up each whole?

____

3. According to the model, how many protons, neutrons, and electrons are contained in an atom of boron?

____

4. According to the model, how many protons, neutrons, and electrons are contained in an atom of helium?

____

5. What pattern do you notice regarding the position of these particles in the models?

____

____

Elements and Atoms: Atomic Matter Through Time

Some diagrams help you compare information. Look at the diagrams below. They show how scientists' views of atoms have changed during the past 200 years. Look carefully at the diagrams. Notice how they differ. Then answer the questions.

Views of Atoms over the Past 200 Years

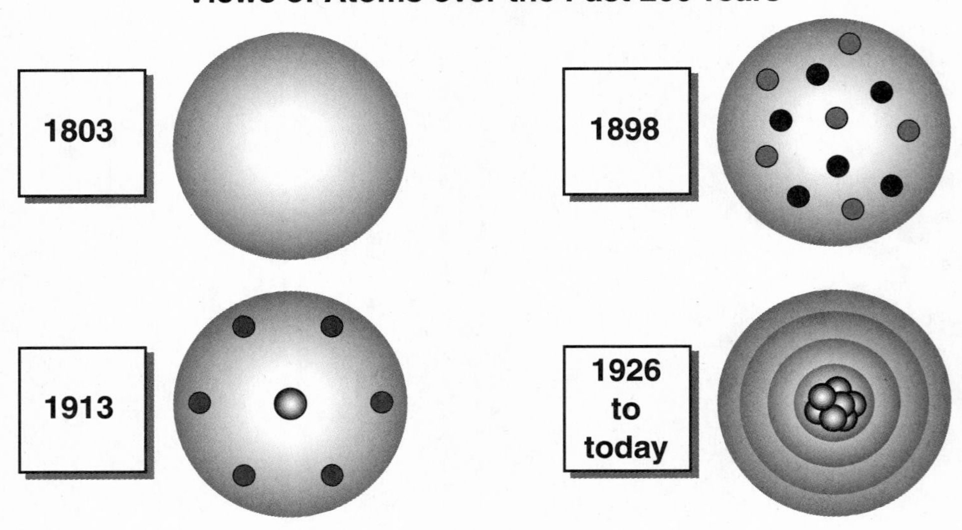

1. Describe the structure of the 1803 model.

____

2. How does the 1898 model differ from the 1803 model?

____

3. How does the 1913 model vary from the 1898 model?

____

____

____

4. How does the present model of the atom vary from the 1913 model?

____

____

____

5. How are all four models alike?

____

Element Lineup

Hypothesize Some elements are more alike than others. How can you tell which are most alike? Different?

Write a **Hypothesis:**

____

____

Materials

- element samples (iron, copper, carbon, aluminum)
- sandpaper
- hand lens

Procedures

1. **Plan** All the samples but one belong to a main group of similar elements. Can you tell which belong? Which does not? Decide how you will start. Write your ideas.

   ____

   ____

   ____

2. **Observe** Use the hand lens to look closely at each sample. Note any differences.

   ____

   ____

3. **Observe** Rub each sample with sandpaper. What can you learn about each?

   ____

   ____

   ____

   ____

   ____

Conclude and Apply

1. **Analyze** Which characteristics help you identify the most similar samples?

____

____

2. **Analyze** Which sample is most different from the others? How can you tell?

____

____

____

Going Further What other property might you study? Write and conduct an experiment.

My Hypothesis Is:

____

____

My Experiment Is:

____

____

My Results Are:

____

____

____

Name ______________________________ CLOZE TEST 2

Elements and Atoms

Fill in the blanks.

Metals make up approximately three-fourths of the ____________. This group can ____________ electricity. Electric wires such as those inside a stereo set or lamp cord are composed of ____________. A rubber covering keeps the ____________ from becoming too hot as electricity travels through them. A poor choice for wires, the metal ____________ would melt if enough electricity went through it. When exposed to water or ____________, some metals change chemically. Iron rusts when combined with ____________. Nonmetals usually have properties ____________ to metals. At room temperature, most nonmetals are all solids or ____________. However, bromine is a(n) ____________ at room temperature.

Elements and Atoms

Match the correct letter with the description.

_____ **1.** a substance that cannot be broken down further into anything simpler

_____ **2.** the smallest particle of an element that has the same chemical properties as the element

_____ **3.** the densest part of an atom where most of its mass is located

_____ **4.** a positively charged particle inside an atom's nucleus

_____ **5.** a particle with no charge located inside an atom's nucleus

_____ **6.** a negatively charged particle that moves around an atom's nucleus

_____ **7.** the number of protons in the atom of an element

_____ **8.** an element that conducts heat and electricity, is shiny, and bendable

_____ **9.** a metallic mixture

a. metal

b. proton

c. alloy

d. nucleus

e. electron

f. element

g. atomic number

h. atom

i. neutron

Answer each question.

10. Before scientists had the correct tools to look inside elements, how did they draw conclusions about the structure of matter?

They observed physical changes and chemical changes.

11. Why is an atom electrically neutral?

____

____

12. In the modern periodic table, what elements are listed in vertical columns?

____

____

13. Why would the walls of many buildings contain copper wires?

____

Investigate How Substances Can Change

Hypothesize Pennies are largely copper. Will a penny turn green, as copper buildings and statues sometimes do?

Write a **Hypothesis:**

____

____

See what happens to a penny in the presence of vinegar.

Materials

- penny
- vinegar
- petri dish
- salt
- clear-plastic cup
- modeling clay
- tweezers
- goggles

Procedures

Safety Wear goggles when you work with vinegar.

1. **Experiment** Place a small wad of modeling clay on the bottom of a petri dish. Wedge a penny in it so that the penny is vertical.
2. Add a small amount of vinegar to the petri dish, and cover it with a clear-plastic cup.
3. **Observe** Describe the color of the penny one hour and three hours later. Describe the color the next day.

   ____

   ____

4. **Experiment** Use the tweezers to transfer the penny to another petri dish. Cover the penny with a vinegar and salt solution. Observe the penny after one hour, three hours, and one day.

   ____

Conclude and Apply

1. **Infer** What kind of change, if any, was observed in step 3? If you saw a change, was it a chemical or physical change? Explain.

   ____

   ____

2. Infer What kind of change, if any, was observed in step 4? If you saw a change, was it a chemical or physical change? Explain.

___

___

___

Going Further: Problem Solving

3. Hypothesize Explain the difference between your observations in steps 3 and 4.

___

___

___

___

___

___

4. Experiment Find a way to test your hypothesis. You might try repeating the activity using water or club soda instead of vinegar.

___

___

Inquiry

Think of your own question related to chemical reactions. What other metals or liquids would you like to test? *Show your plan to your teacher before you try it.*

My Question Is: ___

___

How I Can Test It: ___

___

___

My Results Are: ___

___

Name ________________________________

How Will Liquids Affect a Penny?

Materials

- sheet of blank paper
- water
- 4 new pennies
- salt
- 4 small dishes
- lemon juice

Procedures

1. Divide a sheet of paper into four sections. Label the sections: water, salt water, lemon juice, salt and lemon juice.
2. Place a penny in each of 4 dishes, and place one dish on each of the sections of the paper.
3. Add water to the dish labeled *water*. Add water and salt to the dish labeled *salt water*. Add lemon juice to the dish labeled *lemon juice*. Add lemon juice and salt to the disk labeled *salt and lemon juice*.
4. Observe the dishes. Then set them aside for an hour.
5. After an hour, observe the dishes again. Record your observations.

Dish	Observation
Penny in water	
Penny in salt water	
Penny in lemon juice	
Penny in salt and lemon juice	

Conclude and Apply

1. What did you observe immediately after adding the liquids to the pennies?

   ____

2. What did you observe after an hour?

   ____

   ____

3. Based on your observations, what do you think was happening?

   ____

   ____

Chemical Changes

In this topic you will learn about how atoms link together to form new substances.

Chemical changes produce substances that have different properties. The rusting of iron is a chemical change. When iron rusts, iron atoms link to oxygen atoms. Rust is an example of a compound. A chemical combination of two or more elements is called a **compound.** A compound has its own properties, different from the substances it is made of.

When chemical changes occur, atoms link together in new ways. A link that atoms or atomic-sized particles can form with each other is called a **chemical bond.** Chemical bonds result from electrical attraction between atoms.

When atoms are linked, there is always a number of one kind of atom linked to another. The number can be in a ratio. The ratio in which atoms are bonded together in a compound is shown by a **chemical formula.** A way of using letters and numbers to show how much of each element is in a substance is called a chemical formula.

Atoms of nonmetals attract extra electrons. Most metals have little attraction for extra electrons. When these two types of atoms come in contact, the nonmetallic atoms may be able to “take” electrons from the metallic atoms, resulting in the formation of ions. An **ion** is an electrically charged particle with unequal numbers of protons and electrons. Ions with opposite charges may bond together.

A group of bonded atoms that act like a single particle is called a **molecule.** The molecules of any given substance are always alike. Compounds made of ions are not made of molecules. Instead they are just collections of ions that are held together by opposite charges. Ammonia is made of molecules—salt is made of ions.

A way of describing how a substance changes chemically with other substances is called a **chemical property.** An element’s chemical properties can be predicted from its position in the periodic table. Acids and bases are compounds with different chemical properties. Some acids can be corrosive and some bases can be poisonous. A way to test for acids or bases is to use an indicator, such as litmus paper.

Chemical reactions give off or absorb heat. Chemical reactions that give off heat are said to be **exothermic.** The burning of acetylene gas is an example of an exothermic reaction. In this reaction, energy is released. Chemical reactions that absorb heat are said to be **endothermic.** Endothermic reactions require that a supply of energy be applied.

Many reactions can provide heat. Fossil fuels are commonly burned to provide heat to homes. They are important fuels that date back to ancient organisms of Earth’s past.

Chemical Changes

Fill in the blanks.

How Can Substances Change?

1. Chemical changes produce substances that have new and different ______________.

2. A chemical combination of two or more substances is a(n) ______________.

3. The properties of a compound are different from the ______________ it is made of.

What Happens to Atoms in Chemical Changes?

4. The electrical attraction between atoms forms ______________.

5. The ratio in which atoms are bonded together in a compound is shown by a(n) ______________.

How Do Atoms Form Chemical Bonds?

6. Atoms share electrons in a(n) ______________ bond.

7. In water, covalent bonds join two ______________ atoms to one oxygen atom.

How Else Can Chemical Bonds Form?

8. A particle that has unequal numbers of protons and electrons is a(n) ______________.

9. When a sodium ion and a chloride ion join through a(n) ______________ bond, the compound sodium chloride is produced.

Are All Compounds Made of Molecules?

10. A group of bonded atoms that acts like a single particle is called a(n) ______________.

11. The molecules of any given substance are always ______________.

What Kinds of Chemical Changes Are There?

12. Two elements or compounds join together to make a new compound in a(n) ______________ reaction.

13. A compound breaks apart into simpler substances in a(n) ______________ reaction.

14. One element replaces another element in a compound in a(n) ______________ reaction.

15. The new substances produced through a chemical reaction are called ______________.

How Can We Describe Something Chemically?

16. A way of describing how a substance changes chemically with other substances is a(n) ______________.

17. An element's chemical properties can be predicted from its ______________ in the periodic table.

Why Is Lemon Juice Sour?

18. Sour taste is one common property of ______________ dissolved in water.

19. A substance that changes color in the presence of a test substance is a(n) ______________.

Why Can Milk of Magnesia Taste Blah?

20. Bitter taste is one common property of ______________.

21. In the presence of a base, red litmus turns ______________.

When Do Chemical Reactions Give Off or Absorb Heat?

22. Chemical reactions that give off heat are said to be ______________.

23. Chemical reactions that absorb heat are said to be ______________.

What Are Fossil Fuels?

24. Anything that can be burned to produce heat is a(n) ______________.

25. Chemical changes give you the ______________ you need to live.

Chemical Changes: Covalent Bond

A caption is a sentence or two that provides information about what is shown in a diagram. They help you understand the illustration. Look at the diagrams below. Carefully read the captions. Then answer the questions.

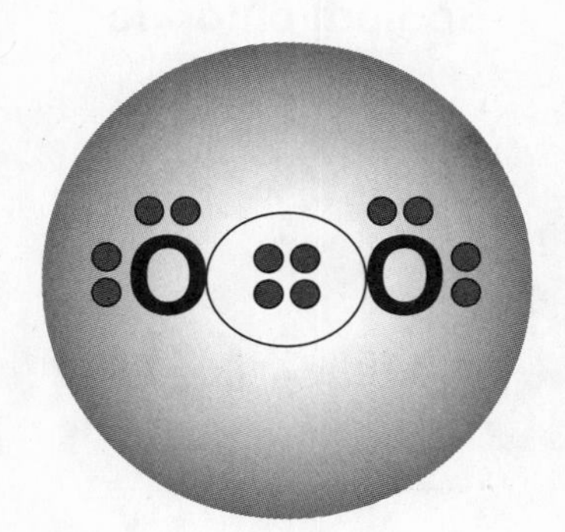

Oxygen atoms in the atmosphere are paired together with covalent bonds. Notice that the atoms share four electrons equally.

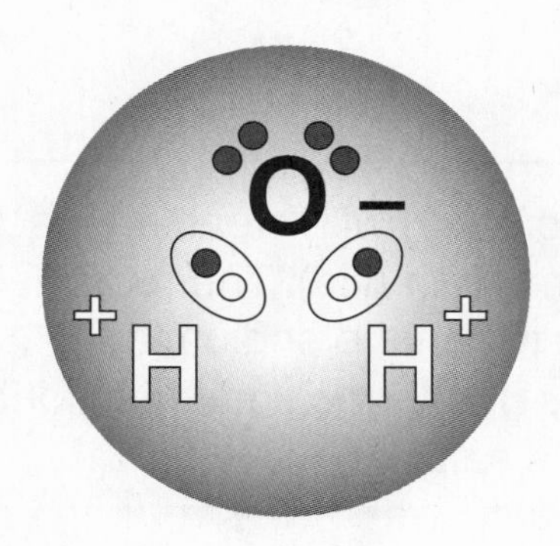

In water, covalent bonds join two hydrogen atoms to an oxygen atom. Oxygen attracts electrons more strongly than hydrogen, which is why the diagram includes plus and minus signs.

1. What kinds of atoms are illustrated?

____

2. What type of bond joins oxygen atoms in the atmosphere?

____

3. What type of bond joins hydrogen and oxygen atoms in water?

____

4. What do the four dark circles found between the two oxygen atoms represent?

____

5. What is the ratio of H to O in a molecule of water? ______________

6. What do the + and – signs represent?

____

____

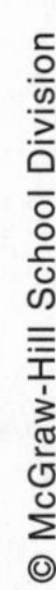

Chemical Changes: Ionic Bond

Some diagrams contain symbols. Each symbol has its own specific meaning. Look at the diagram below. Translate each symbol. Then answer the questions.

Sodium atom **Chlorine atom** **Sodium chloride**

+

A chlorine atom (Cl) will "steal" an electron from a sodium atom (Na). The result is an ionic bond between the sodium and chloride ions. This forms sodium chloride, also known as salt.

1. What does the circle labeled *Na* represent?

____

2. What does the circle labeled *Cl* represent?

____

3. What compound is produced from these atoms?

____

4. What do the two circles between *Na* and *Cl* in the sodium chloride molecule represent?

____

5. How would you read this diagram moving from left to right?

____

Using Numbers and Communicating

Chemical Formulas

You can represent almost any substance with a chemical formula. Here are some simple rules for writing formulas. A chemical formula is a simple way to communicate what a compound is made of. Written correctly it can be understood around the world.

1. The elements with the strongest attraction for extra electrons are written last. Elements that are higher up and farther to the right in the periodic table tend to attract electrons more strongly.
2. For molecules, subscripts indicate the actual number of atoms in each molecule. For example, the formula H_2O indicates a molecule with two hydrogen atoms and one oxygen atom.
3. For ionic compounds, subscripts indicate the simplest ratio of ions present.

Materials

- clay of different colors
- periodic table

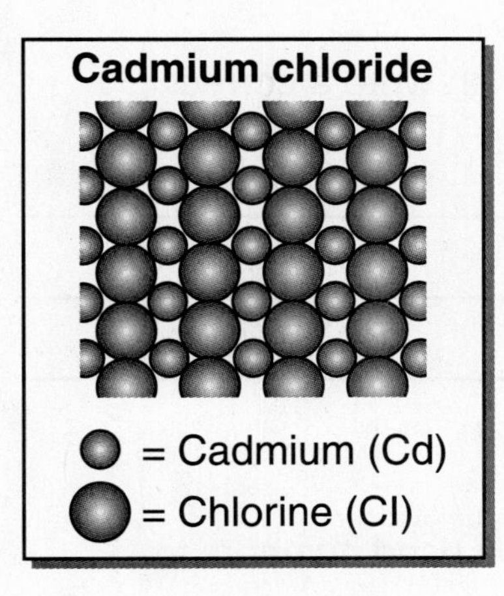

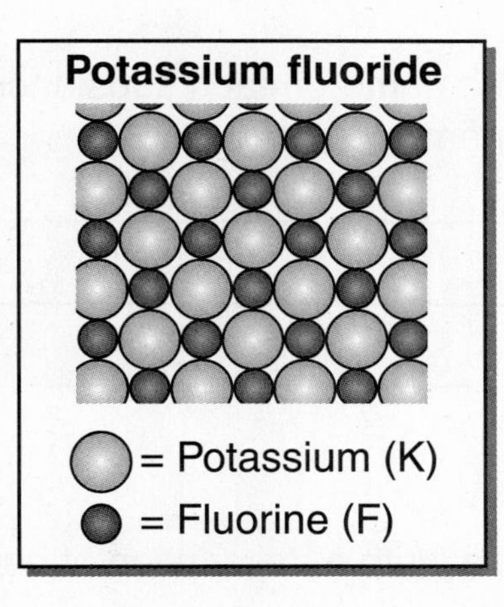

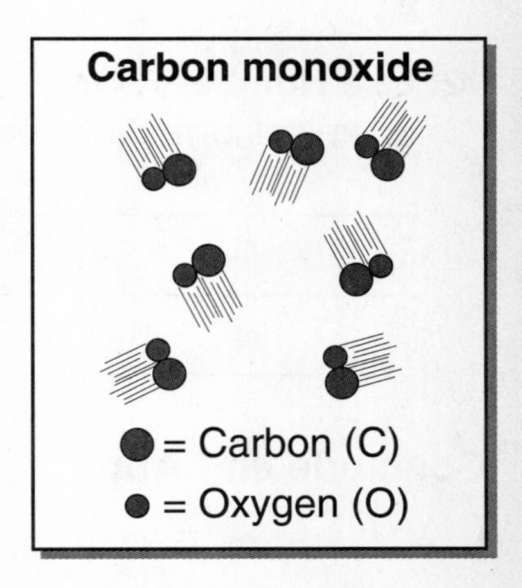

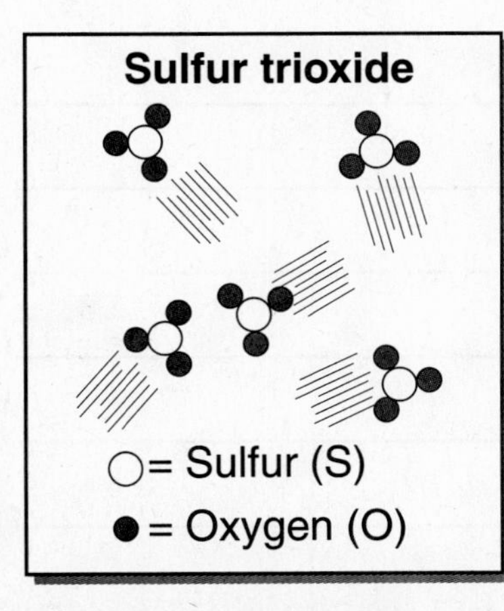

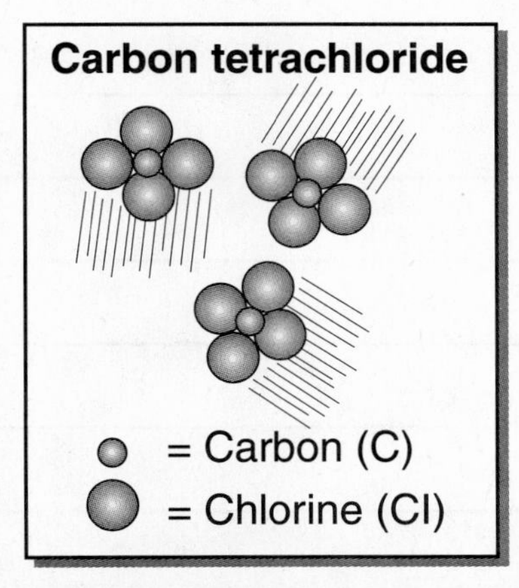

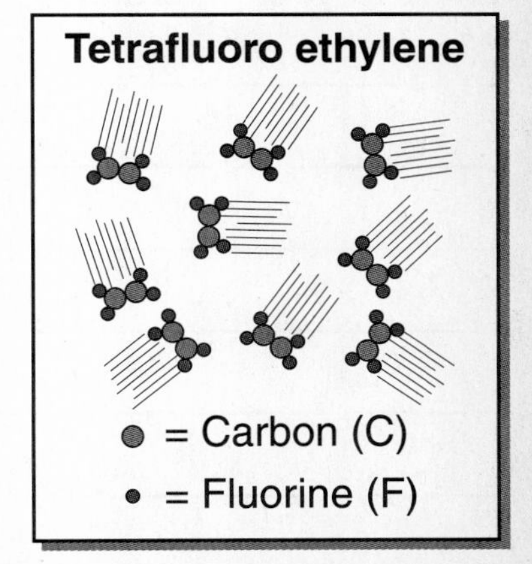

Procedures

1. **Make a Model** The table shows models of several substances. Use clay balls to represent these substances. Use a different color for each element. Draw a diagram of your results in the space provided below.

2. **Use Numbers** Write out the name of each substance. Then write a correct chemical formula by each name.

___

___

___

Conclude and Apply

Use Numbers For each formula write a description of how you used numbers to arrive at your answer.

___

___

___

___

___

___

Chemical Changes

Fill in the blanks.

The original substances in a chemical reaction are called ________________. The ________________ are the new substances produced by the chemical change. Bubbles in soda appear during a(n) ________________ reaction. An example of a(n) ________________ reaction is the rusting of steel wool. During a replacement reaction, one element replaces another in a(n) ________________. Elements' chemical properties can be predicted from their ________________________ positions. Elements in the first column react immediately on contact with ________________. Elements in the last column, called the ________________________, rarely form compounds with other elements. Metals in the ________________ column are more stable than sodium. For this reason, these elements are used to produce ________________.

Chemical Changes

Match the correct letter with the description.

_____ **1.** a chemical combination of two or more elements

_____ **2.** the links that atoms or atomic-sized particles can form with one another

_____ **3.** a way of using letters and numbers to show how much of each element is in a substance

_____ **4.** an electrically charged particle with unequal numbers of protons and electrons

_____ **5.** a group of bonded atoms that acts like a single particle

_____ **6.** a way of describing a substance by how it changes chemically with other substances

_____ **7.** chemical reactions that give off heat

_____ **8.** chemical reactions that absorb energy

_____ **9.** anything that can be burned to produce heat

a. chemical bonds
b. endothermic
c. molecule
d. compound
e. fuel
f. chemical formula
g. exothermic
h. chemical property
i. ion

Answer each question.

10. Why does carbon dioxide have the chemical formula CO_2?

____

____

11. What kind of bonds do nonmetals usually form?

____

12. What kind of bond occurs when an atom of sodium joins an atom of chlorine to form sodium chloride?

____

13. What kind of change occurs when iron rusts?

____

Name ______________________

Properties and Changes

Circle the letter of the best answer.

1. Any solid, liquid, or gas is
   - a. an ion.
   - b. matter.
   - c. solutions.
   - d. weight.

2. The measure of how hard it is to push or pull an object is its
   - a. chemical property.
   - b. density.
   - c. mass.
   - d. volume.

3. To calculate the density of an object, you must know the object's
   - a. length and width.
   - b. mass and volume.
   - c. physical and chemical properties.
   - d. volume and weight.

4. If an object is placed in a less dense liquid or gas, the object will
   - a. expand.
   - b. float.
   - c. shrink.
   - d. sink.

5. Melting point and boiling point are examples of
   - a. chemical changes.
   - b. chemical properties.
   - c. physical properties.
   - d. states of matter.

6. A substance that has a definite shape and volume is classified as a(n)
   - a. gas.
   - b. ion.
   - c. liquid.
   - d. solid.

7. A color change, heat, and light are signs of a
   - a. chemical change.
   - b. mixture.
   - c. physical change.
   - d. solution.

Circle the letter of the best answer.

8. A substance that cannot be broken down into anything simpler is a(n)

a. compound. **b.** element.

c. molecule. **d.** mixtures.

9. The nucleus of an atom contains

a. electrons and neutrons. **b.** electrons and protons.

c. neutrons and protons. **d.** protons and elements.

10. If the atomic number of chlorine is 17, then a chlorine atom contains 17

a. electrons. **b.** metals.

c. neutrons. **d.** protons.

11. An example of a compound is

a. helium. **b.** hydrogen.

c. oxygen. **d.** water.

12. A group of bonded atoms that acts like a single particle is a(n)

a. atom. **b.** element.

c. molecule. **d.** solution.

13. An ion has an electric charge because the particle contains unequal numbers of

a. atoms and molecules. **b.** electrons and protons.

c. molecules and protons. **d.** neutrons and electrons.

14. A reaction that gives off heat is said to be

a. a chemical change. **b.** a physical change.

c. endothermic. **d.** exothermic.

Name ____________________________________

Investigate How You Can Tell Warm from Cold

Hypothesize Is your skin a good tool for measuring warm and cool? Can anything affect the way your skin senses warmth?

Write a **Hypothesis:**

____

____

____

____

____

Test how reliable your sense of touch is in telling temperature.

Materials

- 3 cups or glasses

Procedures

1. Fill glass 1 with warm water, not hot water. Caution: Hot water can burn the skin.
2. Fill glass 2 with room-temperature water.
3. Fill glass 3 with cold water from a refrigerator.
4. **Observe** Hold the three middle fingers of your left hand in the warm water. Hold the three middle fingers of your right hand in the cold water. Record the difference in what you feel.

   ____

   ____

5. **Experiment** Hold your fingers in the same glasses again, as in step 4. Then quickly put both the left and right hand fingers in the room-temperature water. What do you feel in each set of fingers?

   ____

   ____

Conclude and Apply

1. **Hypothesize** When you put both hands in the room-temperature water, did they feel the same? Explain why you felt what you did.

___

___

___

___

___

___

___

2. **Evaluate** Based on your observations, do you think your skin is a reliable way to tell how hot or cold something is?

___

Going Further: Problem Solving

3. **Experiment** Try other ways to repeat this activity to investigate your ideas. For example, you might replace the room-temperature water with warm water—or cool water. Safety is important—use warm, never hot, water.

___

___

Inquiry

Think of your own question related to temperature. Is your sense of touch unreliable in determining the relative warmth of materials other than water?

My Question Is: ___

___

How I Can Test It: ___

___

My Results Are: ___

___

Name ______________________________

Comparing Hot and Cold

Materials

- different types of cloth
- objects made of metal
- paper
- objects made of wood

Procedures

1. Your teacher will give you a variety of objects.
2. Touch each object and decide if it feels warm or cold to the touch. Record your observations.

Warm Objects	Cold Objects

3. Discuss your results with your group. Check to see if there were objects on which group members disagreed.
4. As a class, discuss your results. Make a list of class results.

Conclude and Apply

1. What kinds of objects seemed warm to the touch?

____

____

2. What kinds of objects seemed cold to the touch?

____

____

3. Do you think the objects really were at different temperatures? Explain your answer.

____

____

Temperature and Heat

In this topic you will learn about how heat energy moves from one location to another.

The energy of any moving object is called **kinetic energy.** Energy cannot be created or destroyed. It can only be changed from one form to another. A speeding roller coaster has a great deal of kinetic energy as it reaches the bottom of the first hill. The kinetic energy cannot disappear when it reaches the bottom of the hill. The kinetic energy changes to a new form called potential energy. The energy stored in an object or a material is called **potential energy.**

Molecules in a material move around at different speeds. Taken together they have an average speed. The average speed of the molecules in a material determines the molecules' average kinetic energy. **Temperature** is a measure of the average kinetic energy of the molecules in a material.

Energy always flows from the hotter object to the cooler one. Energy will continue to flow until the two objects reach the same temperature. The energy that flows between objects that have different temperatures is called **heat.**

Heat can move. The transfer of energy by electromagnetic waves is called **radiation.** Objects near room temperature give off mainly infrared radiation, which our eyes cannot see. When objects are heated to about 600°C, they begin to give off visible light.

The spread of molecular motion between areas of different temperatures that are in contact is called **conduction.** Conduction is the only way heat can travel through solids. Another type of heat transfer, called convection, can occur in liquids and gases. **Convection** is the transfer of energy by the flow of a liquid or a gas. In the atmosphere, warmer air carries heat upward. The warm air rises because of its lower density. Cooler air is denser and sinks.

Insulation prevents heat from flowing in or out of a material. A material can be insulated by wrapping it securely with something that is not a good conductor of heat. Air is a very poor conductor of heat and is therefore a good insulator.

Temperature and Heat

Fill in the blanks.

How Can You Tell Warm from Cold?

1. The words *hot* and *cold* are used to describe the ______________ of something.

2. Any moving object has energy due to its ______________.

What Are Two Main Kinds of Energy?

3. The energy of any moving object is called ______________ energy.

4. Energy stored in an object or material is ______________ energy.

5. The amount of energy needed to raise the temperature of 1 gram of water by 1 degree Celsius is one ______________.

So Just What Is Temperature?

6. The average kinetic energy of the molecules in a material is its ______________.

7. An instrument used to measure temperature is a(n) ______________.

Does Energy Flow?

8. Before energy can flow between two objects, there must be a difference in the ______________ of the objects.

9. Energy always flows from a hotter object to a(n) ______________ one.

10. Energy that flows between two objects because they have different temperatures is called ______________.

How Can Heat Move?

11. The transfer of energy by electromagnetic waves is ______________.

12. Objects that absorb electromagnetic radiation receive ______________.

What Are Other Ways Heat Can Move?

13. The movement of energy through direct contact is ____________________.

14. The transfer of heat by the flow of a liquid or a gas is ____________________.

Do Some Materials Warm Faster than Others?

15. Equal masses of different materials have a different temperature change for the same amount of ____________________ absorbed.

16. The particular rate at which a material warms up upon absorbing heat is a(n) ____________________ property that can be used to identify a substance.

17. One gram of liquid ____________________ rises less in temperature than 1 gram of many other substances per calorie of heat absorbed.

How Can We Keep Heat from Going In or Out?

18. Preventing heat from flowing in or out of a material is called ____________________.

19. When you insulate something, you wrap it with a material that is not a good ____________________ of heat.

20. Since air is a poor conductor of ____________________, it adds to the insulating ability of fiberglass.

How Do Insulated Bottles Work?

21. Liquids in an insulated bottle stay at their original ____________________ because heat neither enters nor leaves easily.

22. Microwave ovens use transfer of heat by ____________________ to cook foods.

Name ______________________________

Temperature and Heat: From Hot to Cold

Sometimes diagrams are used to illustrate changes over time. Such diagrams are usually labeled to show how much time has passed. Look at the diagrams below. Read all labels. Then answer the questions.

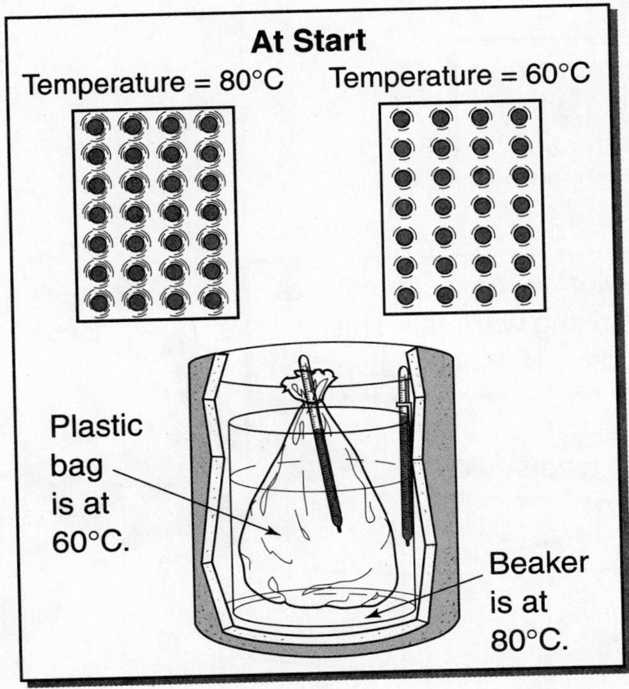

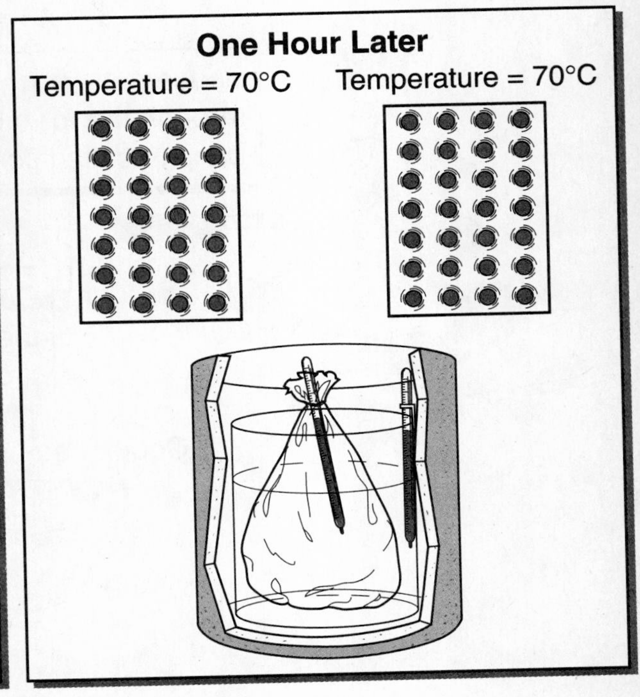

1. How much time has passed between the first and second diagrams? ______________

2. Compare the particles in the first diagram ("At Start").

____

____

3. Compare the particles in the second diagram ("One Hour Later").

____

____

4. What change do the diagrams show?

____

____

5. What might have caused this change?

____

Temperature and Heat: Transferring Heat

Different diagrams placed next to each other on a page are usually related in some way. Look at the two diagrams below. Note what each one represents. Think about how they are related. Then answer the questions.

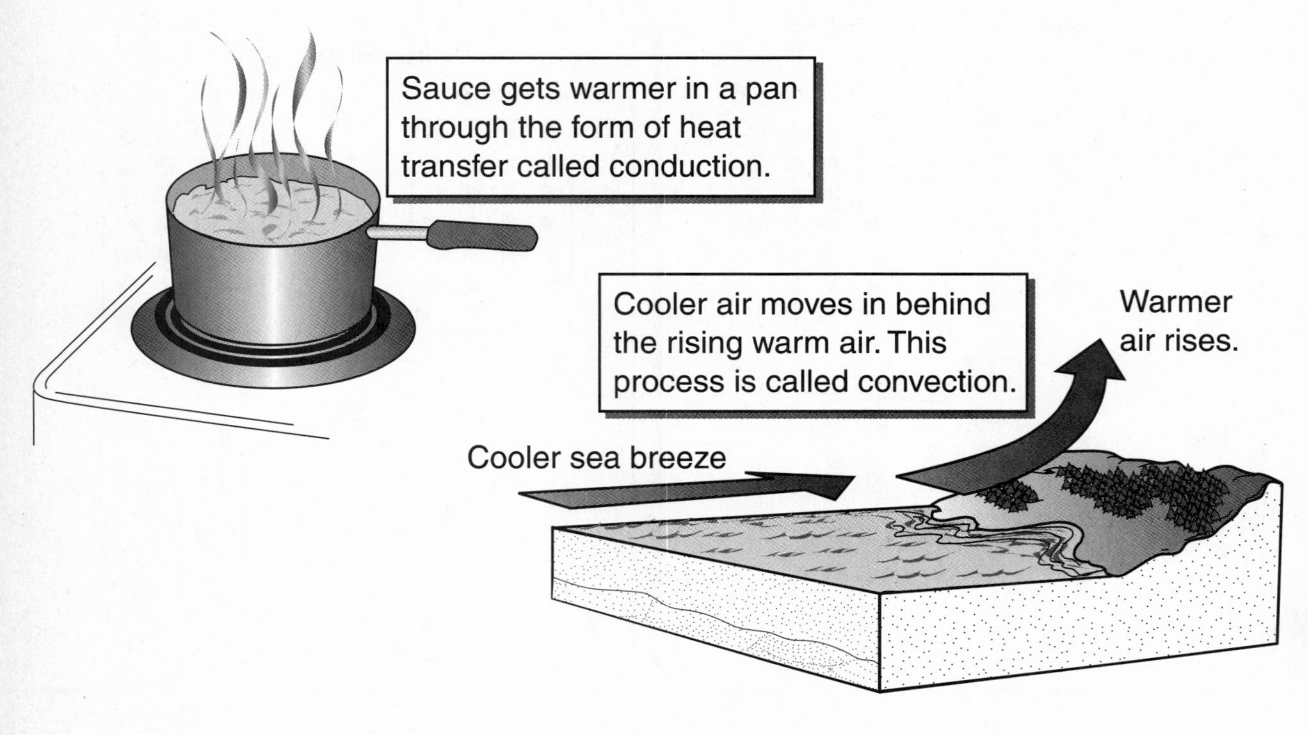

1. Describe what appears to be happening in the pan.

____

____

2. What is this process called? ______________

3. Describe what appears to be happening to the air over the land.

____

____

4. What do the arrows represent? ______________________

5. What is this process called? ______________

6. How are these two diagrams related?

____

____

Separating and Controlling Variables

Which Warms Faster—Water or Sand?

Perhaps you have visited a sandy beach on a sunny day and noticed that the sand is too hot to walk on, while the water feels comfortable. Does sand warm up faster than water for the same amount of heat? Design an experiment to answer this question.

In an experiment a variable is something that can affect the outcome. For example, in testing how rapidly water and sand warm up, the length of time the materials are heated would affect their temperature. To make the test "fair", you would have to heat both materials for the same length of time. Making sure that a variable is the same for all samples being tested is called *controlling the variable*.

Materials

- desk lamp
- thermometers
- sand
- water
- 2 containers

Procedures

1. **Hypothesize** Which warms up faster—water or sand? Write a hypothesis.

____

____

____

2. **Use Variables** Make a list of the variables that could affect how rapidly sand and water warm up when heated.

____

____

3. Plan Write a procedure to compare how fast water and sand warm up for the same amount of heat. Have your teacher check your plan.

____

____

____

____

____

____

____

4. If possible carry out your procedure. Write a report that describes your results on a separate piece of paper.

Conclude and Apply

1. Communicate Summarize your results. Use graphs to show temperature changes of the two substances over time.

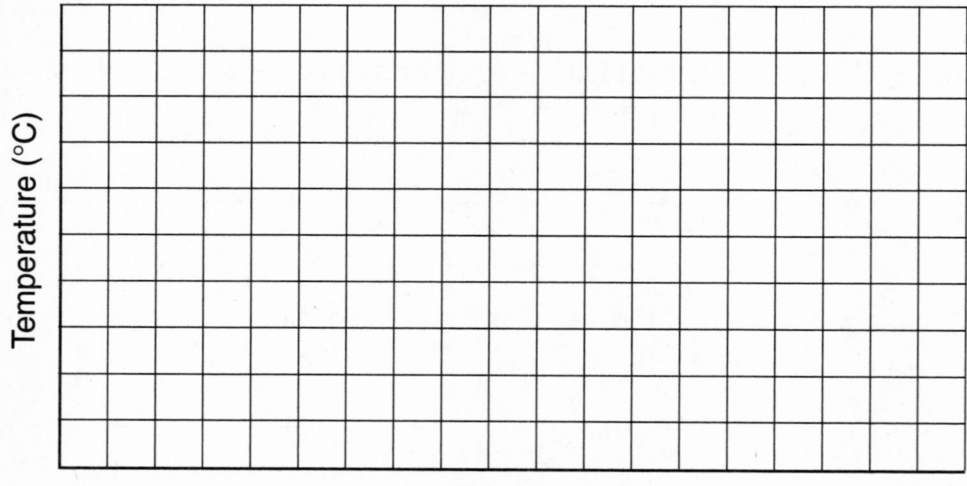

2. Explain your results.

____

____

Name ______________________________ CLOZE TEST 4

Temperature and Heat

Fill in the blanks.

The transfer of energy by electromagnetic waves is called ____________. These waves can travel through space from the ____________ to Earth. On Earth, radiation includes visible, ____________, and ____________ waves. Our eyes cannot see infrared radiation. Objects give off visible light when they are ____________ to 600°C. As the temperature rises to thousands of degrees, the light becomes ____________. When objects absorb electromagnetic energy, they might change from one state of ____________ to another, such as snow melting in sunshine. Heat can travel through solids by ____________. It can travel through liquids and gases by another heat transfer called ____________. For example, in the ____________, warm air rises upward.

Temperature and Heat

Match the correct letter with the description.

_____ **1.** the energy of a moving object

_____ **2.** energy stored in an object or material

_____ **3.** the average kinetic energy of the molecules in a material

_____ **4.** an instrument that measures temperature

_____ **5.** energy that flows between objects that have different temperatures

_____ **6.** the movement of energy through direct contact

_____ **7.** the transfer of energy by the flow of a liquid or a gas

_____ **8.** preventing heat from flowing in or out of a material

_____ **9.** the transfer of energy by electromagnetic waves

a. heat
b. convection
c. kinetic energy
d. conduction
e. temperature
f. radiation
g. thermometer
h. potential energy
i. insulation

Answer each question.

10. Describe how energy flows between hotter and cooler objects.

____

____

11. What is the only way heat can travel through solids?

____

____

12. Why would air add to the insulating ability of fiberglass?

____

13. Give one example of radiation.

____

14. Does the same temperature change take place when equal masses of different materials absorb heat?

____

Name ______________________________

Investigate What Heat Can Do to Matter

Hypothesize How does heat affect a gas? How might it affect matter in general?

Write a **Hypothesis:**

____

____

See how the size of a balloon is affected by hot and cold.

Materials

- 2 identical balloons
- pan of ice water
- pan of warm water
- modeling compound or clay (optional)

Procedures

1. Blow up the balloons so that both are the same size. Tie each balloon so that no air escapes.
2. **Use Variables** Put one balloon aside, away from either pan of water.
3. **Experiment** Put the second balloon into the warm water for five minutes.
4. **Compare** Remove the balloon from the water. Compare its size with the size of the first. Record your observations.

   ____

5. **Experiment** Place the second balloon in the ice water for five minutes. Repeat step 4.

   ____

Conclude and Apply

1. **Explain** Why did you put the first balloon aside?

   ____

2. **Communicate** What happened when you put the balloon in warm water? In ice water?

   ____

   ____

3. **Draw Conclusions** How does heat affect a gas?

____

Going Further: Problem Solving

4. **Hypothesize** How might your results change if you used two equal cubes of modeling compound or clay instead of the balloons? How would one cube compare to the other if one was heated in warm water? Cooled in ice water? Write a hypothesis. Test your ideas.

____

____

____

____

Inquiry

Think of your own question related to heat and matter. Test the effect of heat or cold on a material of your choice.

My Question Is:

____

____

How I Can Test It:

____

____

____

____

My Results Are:

____

____

Heating Air

Materials

- hot plate
- pan of water
- heat-resistant bottle with narrow mouth
- balloon

Procedures

 **Safety** Be careful when handling the hot plate.

1. Place a pan of water on a hot plate.
2. Stretch a balloon to make it easier to inflate. Put the balloon on the neck of the bottle. Make sure the balloon is securely stretched over the top of the bottle.
3. Place the bottle in the pan of water. Turn on the hot plate and slowly heat the water. *Caution: Do not heat the water all the way to the boiling point.* Observe what happens to the balloon.
4. Turn off the hot plate and allow the water to cool. Observe what happens to the balloon as the water cools.

Conclude and Apply

1. What did you observe as the water was heated?

____

____

2. What did you observe as the water cooled?

____

____

3. Based on your observations, what generalization can you make about the effect of heat on a gas?

____

____

Temperature, Heat, and Matter

In this topic you will learn about how heat transfer causes changes in matter.

The expansion of matter when its temperature is raised is called **thermal expansion.** As the temperature of a material is raised, its particles move about faster. Each particle moves over a larger region. As a result, the material that is made up of the particles increases in volume.

Gases are made of tiny particles in rapid motion. The molecules hit each other and the wall of their container. All of the countless tiny hits of particles add up to create a push called pressure. **Pressure** is the force on each unit of area of surface.

When heat is applied to a solid, the particles begin to vibrate faster and faster as their temperature rises. Eventually the particles move fast enough to break free of the forces holding them in place. This process is called melting. **Melting** is the change of a solid into a liquid.

The particles in a liquid remain close together because of the forces of attraction. If heat is supplied to a liquid, the particles move faster. At some point they will move enough to escape the liquid and form a gas. The change of a liquid to a gas as molecules break free from each other is called **vaporization.**

If energy is removed from a gas, the particles slow down. The change of a gas into a liquid as molecules attract each other is called **condensation.** If energy is removed from a liquid the particles will eventually be locked back into a fixed position. The change of a liquid to a solid is called **freezing.**

The temperature of a substance does not change while a change of state occurs. The energy flowing into a substance breaks the attraction between the particles. It does not also speed them up.

The temperature of a vaporizing liquid stays unchanged while a liquid is boiling, even though the liquid is being heated. In a similar way, the energy it takes to break the attraction in melting or vaporization must be removed when particles bond back together during condensation or freezing.

The formation of bubbles of vapor that escape from a liquid that is being heated is called **boiling.** Liquids may also turn to gas at lower temperatures when particles vaporize at the surface. The vaporization of molecules from the surface of a liquid is called **evaporation.**

Concepts of conduction, convection, and radiation are very important in our everyday life. Homes can be heated using convection, conduction, and radiation, as in the case of steam heating. Buidings can also be heated by convection alone using a forced-air heating system. Cars use gases to push on pistons and refrigerators move heat from foods inside to the air outside.

Name ______________________________

Temperature, Heat, and Matter

Fill in the blanks.

What Can Heat Do to Matter?

1. The expansion of matter when its temperature is raised is called ______________________.
2. Before a bimetallic strip turns a thermostat off, heat must cause one side of the metal to ______________ more than the other side.

What Causes Thermal Expansion?

3. As the temperature of a solid, liquid, or gas is raised, the particles of the substance move ______________.
4. Heat causes molecules of a substance to vibrate rapidly which causes the substance to increase in ______________.
5. Different materials expand or ______________ with changing temperature at their own particular rates.

How Do Gas Molecules Push on Surfaces?

6. The force on each unit of area of a surface is called ______________.
7. After air is pumped into a bicycle tire, the pressure inside the tire becomes ______________.

What Happens When a Gas Gets Hot?

8. As a gas is heated, the speed at which the gas particles travel ______________.
9. The volume of a gas increases when its ______________ is raised while keeping its pressure constant.

How Can Heat Change Matter?

10. Adding or removing ______________ causes matter to change from one state to another.
11. The changing of a solid to a liquid is ______________.
12. The change of a liquid to a gas is ______________.

How Can Cooling Change Matter?

13. The change of a gas into a liquid as molecules attract each other is

________________.

14. The change of a liquid into a solid is called ________________.

15. When bubbles of vapor escape from a liquid as a result of heating,

________________ occurs.

16. The vaporization of molecules from the surface of a liquid is ________________.

What Are Two Ways to Heat a Room?

17. In a steam heating system, water first changes state from a liquid to

a(n) ________________.

18. The stored heat is then released as water ________________ from

steam into a liquid.

19. Air in a room is heated by ________________ when it comes in

contact with the hot pipes of the radiator.

20. Forced-air heating systems do not involve a change of ________________

found in steam heating systems.

How Can Gases Drive a Car?

21. Inside a car engine, heat from burning ________________ warms gases

produced by the burning to high temperatures.

22. These gases then push on ________________ which propel the car.

How Can Gases Keep Food Cold?

23. A refrigerator moves heat from foods and beverages inside to the

________________ outside.

24. Ice absorbs heat by ________________.

Name ______________________________ STUDY AID 5

Temperature, Heat, and Matter: Changes of State

Some diagrams show a sequence of events. The first item shown occurs first, the second item shown occurs next, and so on. Look at the diagram below. Pay careful attention to the order in which each event is shown. Then answer the questions.

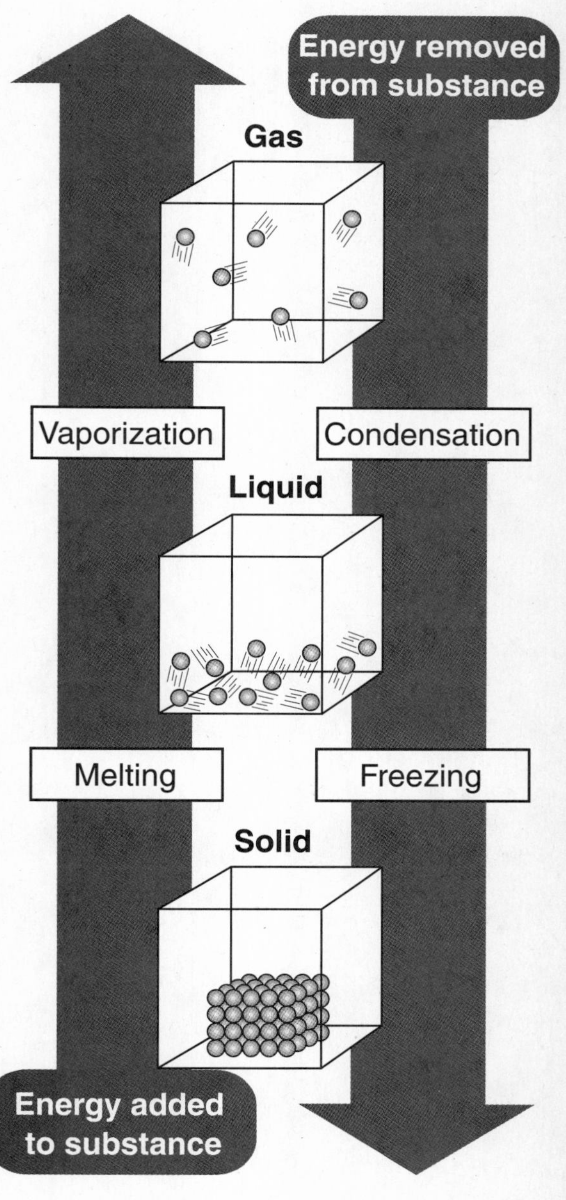

1. What cause-and-effect relationship is illustrated by the diagram?

____

____

2. What does the large arrow on the left side of the diagram represent?

____

____

3. What does the large arrow on the right side of the diagram represent?

____

____

4. What process changes a solid to a liquid?

____

5. What process changes a liquid to a gas?

____

6. What process changes a liquid to a solid?

____

7. What processes occur when energy is removed from a substance?

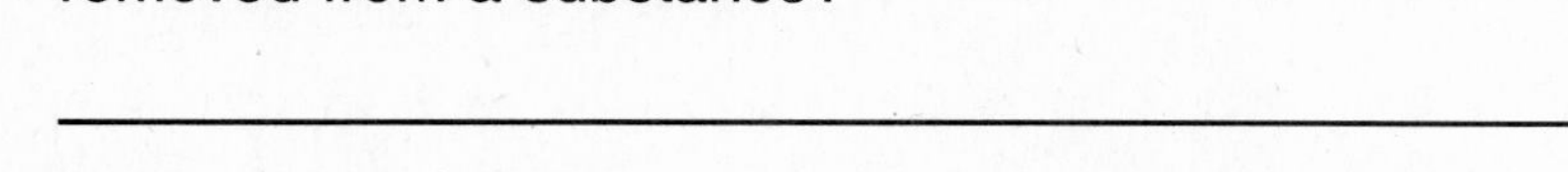

____

8. What processes occur when energy is added to a substance?

____

Color Swirl

Hypothesize Can you model a steam-heating process?

Write a **Hypothesis:**

____

____

Materials

- food-colored ice cube (heavily colored)
- 250-mL beaker three-fourths filled with warm water
- plastic tablespoon
- thermometer

Procedures

1. **Make a Model** Use the tablespoon to hold the food-colored ice cube. Using the tablespoon, slowly and gently lower the ice cube into the warm water. Keep the water in the beaker as still as possible.
2. **Observe** Watch the beaker for several minutes. Describe what you see beginning to happen.

   ____

   ____

3. **Measure** Measure the water temperature at the bottom, the middle and just below the surface. Record your data.

   ____

   ____

4. Repeat step 3 after several minutes.

   ____

   ____

   ____

Conclude and Apply

Infer What do you see in the beaker? Why is it happening? Be sure your idea is supported by all your data.

Going Further How else could you model air flow? Write and conduct an experiment

My Hypothesis Is:

My Experiment Is:

My Results Are:

Name ______________________________ STUDY AID

Temperature, Heat, and Matter: Four-Stroke Engine Cycle

Certain diagrams illustrate the steps in a complex process. Look at the diagrams below. They show parts of the four-stroke engine cycle. Read all labels and captions. Then answer the questions.

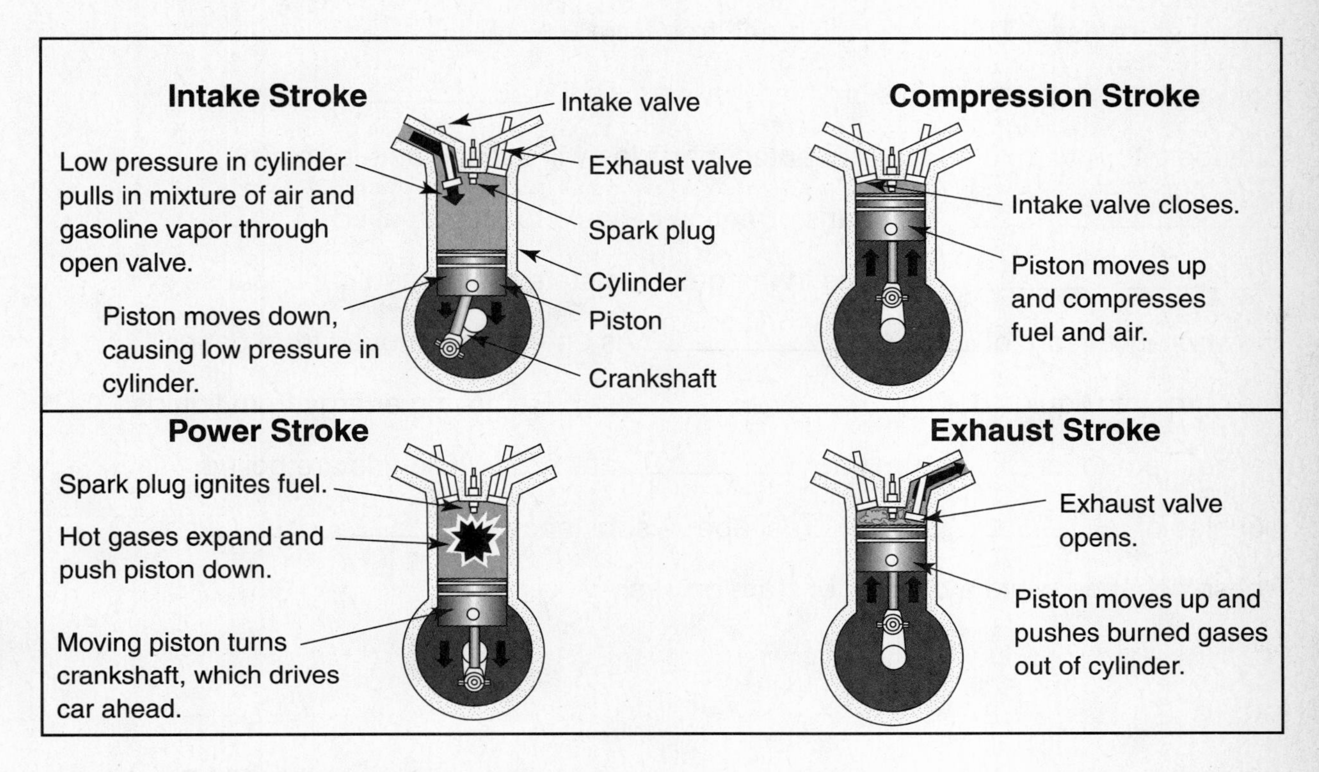

1. What are the four strokes called?

____

2. During which stroke does the intake valve close? ______________________________

3. During which stroke does the exhaust valve open? ______________________________

4. During which stroke are air and gasoline vapor pulled into the engine?

____

5. During which stroke does a moving piston turn the crankshaft?

____

6. What happens immediately after a spark plug ignites fuel?

____

7. What causes fuel and air to compress in the engine?

____

Temperature, Heat, and Matter

Fill in the blanks.

When a solid is heated, particles ________________ rapidly as their temperature rises. Then particles break free from the ________________ holding them in place. In this process, called ________________, solids change into liquids. If a liquid is heated, particles will escape and form a(n) ________________. This transformation of liquid to gas is called ________________. Particles in the gaseous state are spread out because they have freedom of ________________. As energy is removed from gases, they turn into liquids during ________________. Removing energy from liquids cause them to freeze, or turn into ________________. If liquids are boiled, bubbles of ________________ escape. A substance's ________________ doesn't change while a change of state occurs.

Temperature, Heat, and Matter

Match the correct letter with the description.

_____ **1.** the expansion of matter when its temperature is raised

_____ **2.** the force on each unit of the area of a surface

_____ **3.** the change of a solid into a liquid

_____ **4.** the change of a liquid to a gas

_____ **5.** the change of a gas into a liquid

_____ **6.** the change of a liquid into a solid

_____ **7.** when bubbles of vapor escape from a liquid as a result of heating

_____ **8.** the vaporization of molecules from the surface of a liquid

a. vaporization
b. freezing
c. evaporation
d. thermal expansion
e. pressure
f. melting
g. boiling
h. condensation

Answer each question.

9. What creates the pressure inside a bicycle tire?

____

10. What happens to the volume of a gas when its temperature is raised and its pressure is kept constant?

____

11. What happens to the temperature of a substance while a change of state occurs? ________________

12. What is the main way ice absorbs heat?

____

13. How is energy transferred in a steam heating system?

____

14. How does a refrigerator keep foods and beverages cool?

____

____

Investigate How to Use Energy from the Sun

Hypothesize How can you use the Sun's energy for useful purposes, such as to cook food?

Write a **Hypothesis:**

___

___

See how well sunlight can heat food.

Materials

- white construction paper
- unwaxed paper cups
- a peeled apple
- black construction paper
- transparent tape
- aluminum foil

Procedures

1. Place the aluminum foil on top of the white construction paper. The shiny side of the foil should be facing up.
2. Roll the paper and foil into a cone with the bottom narrow enough to fit into the paper cup. Tape the cone so that the cone keeps its shape.
3. Line the inside of one paper cup with black construction paper.
4. Insert the second paper cup into the first. The black construction paper should now be between the two cups.
5. Place small pieces of peeled apple on the bottom of the second cup.
6. Insert the cone, narrow end first, into the second cup and tape it in place.
7. Place the cone in direct sunlight for two hours. Also place small pieces of peeled apple in direct sunlight, next to the cup.

Conclude and Apply

1. **Observe** Look at the pieces of apple every half-hour for two hours. Compare the apple pieces inside the cup and the apple pieces next to the cup.

___

___

...lyze What caused the differences you observed? How do you think the cone works?

____

____

____

Going Further: Problem Solving

3. Plan Would other food items show the same results? Write a hypothesis. How would you test it?

____

____

____

____

____

____

Inquiry

Think of your own question related to solar energy. How hot do solar ovens need to be to cook food?

My Question Is:

____

____

How I Can Test It:

____

____

My Results Are:

____

____

Capturing Solar Energy

Materials

- boxes
- glue
- magnifying glass
- timer
- pieces of cardboard
- aluminum foil
- marshmallows
- thermometer
- tape
- scissors
- pencil
- towels

Procedures

1. Work with a group to design a solar cooker. Discuss with your group ways to capture the Sun's energy and concentrate it on an object. Also discuss how you can test the cooker to evaluate your design.
2. Make a sketch of your group's plan below. Show the plan to your teacher before you begin to construct your solar cooker.
3. After you receive approval from your teacher, construct your solar cooker.
4. On a sunny day, take your cooker outdoors and test it.

Conclude and Apply

1. What method did your group decide to use to concentrate the Sun's energy?

____

____

2. What method did your group agree to use as a test of the cooker?

____

____

3. Was your design successful? If not, how could you modify your design to make it work better?

____

____

Sources of Energy

In this topic you will learn about how alternate sources of energy may be utilized.

Most living things obtain their energy directly or indirectly from the Sun. Scientists have developed materials made mainly of silicon that produce electrons when stuck by light. When layered properly, these materials can be made into solar cells. A **solar cell** is a device that generates an electric current from sunlight.

Fossil fuels were once living plants and animals. Matter from plants and animals living today can produce energy and help conserve fossil fuels. New methods allow us to change both plant and animal materials into high quality fuels. Getting energy from plant and animal materials by changing them into high-quality fuels is called **biomass conversion.**

Atomic nuclei can produce energy in a nuclear reaction. The splitting of a nucleus with a large mass into two nuclei with smaller masses is a nuclear reaction called **nuclear fission.** The nucleus is split when struck by a slow moving neutron. Neutrons that are released by one splitting atom can strike additional nuclei and make them split. These nuclei release several more neutrons and start a reaction that is kept going by products of the reaction called a **chain reaction.**

Energy can also be released when nuclei with smaller masses merge to make a nucleus with a larger mass. This process is called **nuclear fusion.** Nuclear fusion reactions only occur at very high temperatures. In nature, temperatures great enough for nuclear fusion to happen are found in the cores of stars.

The kinetic energy of falling water can be used to turn a wheel. This principle can be used to generate electricity. When electricity is produced by the use of flowing water, it is called **hydroelectricity.** Hydroelectricity is really a form of solar energy. Presently the U.S. gets about 15 percent of its electricity from hydroelectricity.

At an electric power plant, separate cooling water is used to condense the exhaust steam from the turbines. This water warms up as it cools the steam. If the warmed water were to be released into a river or lake, the increase in temperature would harm the water dwelling plants and animals. The excess heating of the environment is called **thermal pollution.**

Sources of Energy

Fill in the blanks.

How Can the Sun's Energy Be Used?

1. Plants convert the Sun's energy into chemical energy stored in compounds called ____________.
2. The Sun's energy heats a fluid as it passes through pipes in a(n) ____________ solar heating system.
3. Heat from the Sun is stored in a thick wall in a(n) ____________ solar heating system.

How Can Sunlight Be Turned into Electricity?

4. A device that generates an electric current from sunlight is a(n) ____________.
5. Some power plants use mirrors to focus the Sun's rays onto a collector where water is heated to ____________.

Why Are Fossil Fuels Called Fossil Fuels?

6. Coal, oil, and ____________ give off large amounts of heat when burned.
7. Fossils fuels are examples of ____________ resources because they take millions of years to form.

Can Modern Plant and Animal Matter Give Us Energy?

8. Getting energy from plant and animal materials by changing them into high-quality fuels is called ____________.
9. The fuels produced through biomass conversion are ____________ resources.

How Can Atomic Nuclei Produce Energy by Splitting?

10. The splitting of a nucleus with a large mass into two nuclei with smaller masses is called ____________.

11. A reaction that is kept going by products of the reaction is called a(n) ____________________.

12. Because the forces in an atomic nucleus are very strong, the energy released in a nuclear fission chain reaction is much greater than the energy produced by ____________________ reactions.

How Can Atomic Nuclei Produce Energy by Merging?

13. Nuclei with smaller masses are merged into a nucleus with a larger mass in a(n) ____________________ reaction.

14. Nuclear fusion reactions can only occur at very high ____________________.

How Can We Use Nuclear Fission to Make Electricity?

15. A large number of power plants use a(n) ____________________ to produce electricity.

16. Most nuclear power plants use ____________________ as a nuclear fuel.

Which Is Better—Fission or Fusion?

17. Waste products of nuclear fission stay highly ____________________ for thousands of years.

18. Researchers have not yet succeeded in developing a working fusion reactor due to the high ____________________ needed to keep fusion going.

How Can We Capture Energy from Wind?

19. Wind is a form of ____________________ energy.

How Can Falling Water Give Us Energy?

20. The use of flowing water to generate electricity is called ____________________.

How Can Fossil Fuels Be Used to Make Electricity?

21. The first change of state that occurs when making electricity from fossil fuels is changing liquid water to ____________________.

How Do Electric Power Plants Control Pollution?

22. The excess heating of the environment is called ____________________.

Name ______________________________

Sources of Energy: Solar Heating Systems

Sometimes, arrows are used to link parts of a diagram with their labels. Look at the diagrams below. Follow the path of each arrow to connect the diagram part and label. Then answer the questions.

An Active Solar Heating System

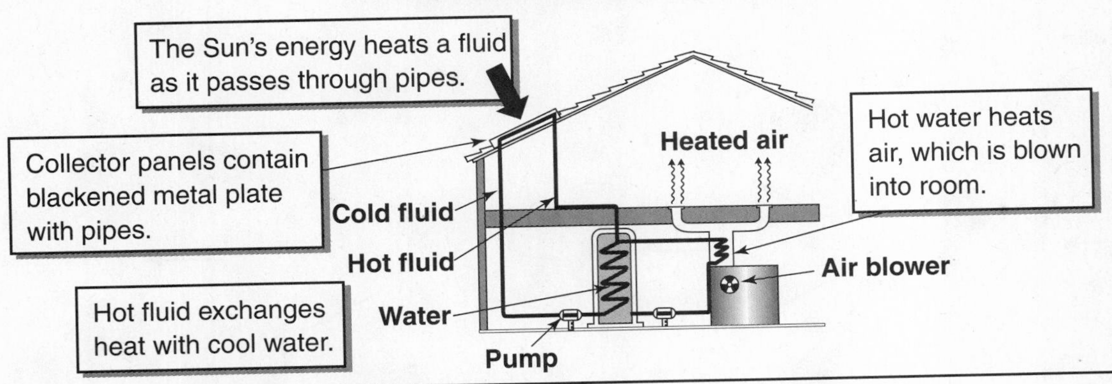

A Passive Solar Heating System

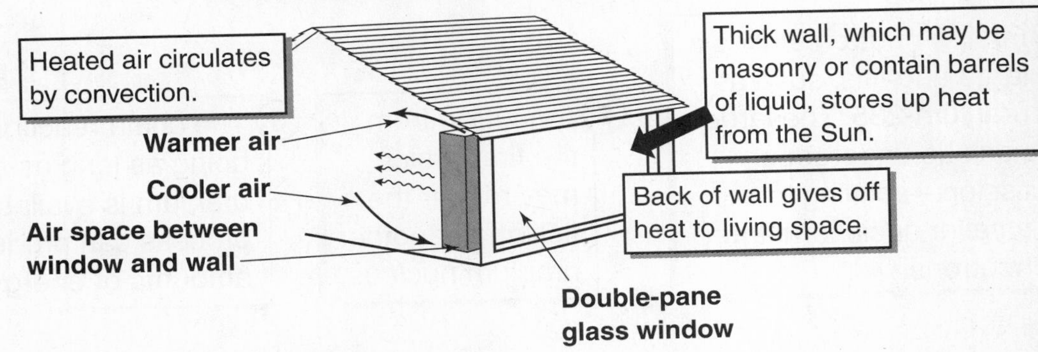

1. What do the diagrams compare?

____

2. What is the source of energy for both diagrams? ______________

3. How does the active solar heating system provide heated air?

____

4. How does the passive solar heating system provide heated air?

____

____

5. What do the wavy lines represent in both systems? ______________

6. How are the final products of these systems alike?

____

Sources of Energy: A Nuclear Chain Reaction

Many processes are dynamic. They involve a great deal of movement. Diagrams of such processes use arrows to indicate motion. Look at the diagram below. Follow the arrows. Then answer the questions.

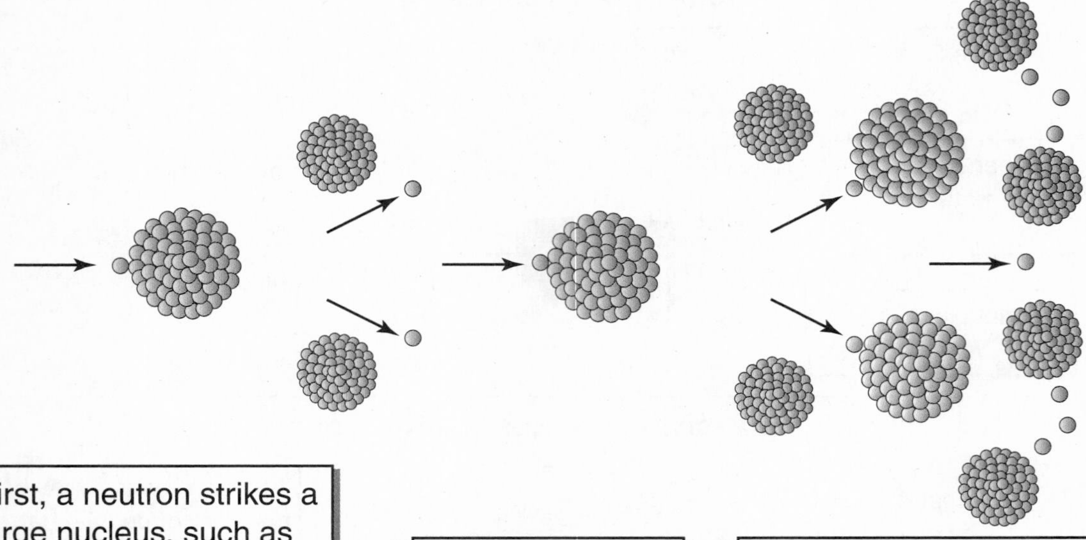

(1) First, a neutron strikes a large nucleus, such as uranium-235. The large nucleus undergoes fission—splitting into smaller nuclei and three neutrons.

(2) A neutron from the first fission may trigger the fission of another uranium nucleus.

(3) The chain reaction will keep going as long as enough uranium is available. The process can produce huge amounts of energy.

1. What process is illustrated by the diagram?

____

2. What does the large, spherical structure represent?

____

3. What does the small sphere represent? ______________

4. What happens when the neutron strikes the nucleus?

____

5. What do the series of arrows represent?

____

____

Name ___

A Chain Reaction

Hypothesize How can you use everyday materials to model a nuclear chain reaction?

Write a **Hypothesis:**

___

___

___

Materials

- everyday materials

Procedures

1. **Plan** Decide on everyday materials that you can use. You might choose foam balls, dried beans, or squares of colored paper to model the nuclei and neutrons. You could present your model on a poster, in a diorama, or as an activity involving your classmates. Record your choice of materials and what they will represent.

___

___

___

2. **Make a Model** With your teacher's approval, build your model. Your teacher may ask you to write an explanation of the model or to discuss the model with the class.

___

___

___

___

Name ______________________________

Conclude and Apply

Evaluate In what ways was your model successful? In what ways was it not successful?

____

____

Going Further How else could you model the reaction? Write and conduct an experiment.

My Hypothesis Is:

____

____

My Experiment Is:

____

____

____

____

My Results Are:

____

____

____

Name ______________________________ CLOZE TEST 6

Sources of Energy

Fill in the blanks.

Wind is a type of solar ______________. It is created by the uneven ______________ of Earth's surface by the Sun. Windmills have been used on farms to pump ______________ and grind grain. Some remote areas also used wind-powered ______________. The need for these lessened when electric companies strung ______________ across America. On wind farms, wind is converted into electricity using large wind ______________. The ______________ energy of falling water can be harnessed to turn a wheel. Flowing water is used to generate electricity in a process called ______________. This method causes little ______________ and is readily available. However, building large ______________ can damage the environment.

Name ______________________________

Sources of Energy

Match the correct letter with the description.

_____ **1.** plants convert the Sun's energy into chemical energy stored in these

_____ **2.** fossil fuels

_____ **3.** how plant and animal materials are changed into high-quality fuels

_____ **4.** the fuels produced from biomass conversion

_____ **5.** the splitting of a nucleus with a large mass into two nuclei with smaller masses

_____ **6.** when nuclei with smaller masses are merged to make a nucleus with a larger mass

_____ **7.** nuclear plants use fission chain reactions to produce this

_____ **8.** the use of flowing water to generate electricity

_____ **9.** the excess heating of the environment

_____ **10.** when products of a reaction keep the reaction going

a. nuclear fusion

b. biomass conversion

c. chain reaction

d. renewable resources

e. electricity

f. nonrenewable resources

g. hydroelectrical energy

h. nuclear fission

i. thermal pollution

j. carbohydrates

Answer each question.

11. What can a solar cell generate from sunlight?

____

12. Why are coal, oil, and natural gas good fuels?

____

____

13. What kinds of temperature are required for a nuclear fusion reaction to take place?

____

____

Temperature, Heat, and Energy

Circle the letter of the best answer

1. The energy of a moving object is called

a. kinetic energy.
b. motion.
c. potential energy.
d. radiant energy.

2. Energy stored in an object or material is

a. heat.
b. insulation.
c. kinetic energy.
d. potential energy.

3. The average kinetic energy of the molecules in a material is

a. convection.
b. heat.
c. joules.
d. temperature.

4. Heat is energy that flows between objects that have

a. different temperatures.
b. equal mass.
c. similar volume.
d. the same boiling point.

5. The transfer of energy by electromagnetic waves is

a. conduction.
b. convection.
c. radiation.
d. thermal expansion.

6. Conduction is the only way that heat can travel between

a. air.
b. gases.
c. liquids.
d. solids.

7. The transfer of energy by the flow of a liquid or gas is

a. conduction.
b. convection.
c. radiation.
d. vaporization.

Circle the letter of the best answer.

8. Preventing heat from flowing in or out of a material is called

a. conduction. **b.** convection.

c. insulation. **d.** melting.

9. The vaporization of molecules from the surface of a liquid is

a. condensation. **b.** evaporation.

c. freezing. **d.** melting.

10. A gas changes into a liquid through

a. condensation. **b.** convection.

c. evaporation. **d.** vaporization.

11. The splitting of a nucleus with a large mass into two nuclei with smaller masses is called

a. biomass conversion. **b.** hydroelectricity.

c. nuclear fission. **d.** nuclear fusion.

12. A device that generates electric current from sunlight is a(n)

a. active solar heating system. **b.** nuclear reactor.

c. passive solar heating system. **d.** solar cell.

13. The merging of nuclei with smaller masses into a nucleus with a larger mass is called

a. biomass conversion. **b.** chain reactions.

c. nuclear fusion. **d.** thermal pollution.

14. The fuels produced through biomass conversion are

a. fossil fuels. **b.** nonrenewable resources.

c. renewable resources. **d.** solar cells.

Name ________________ EXPLORE ACTIVITY 1
Page 1

Investigate What Things Float on Others

Hypothesize How can the fact that a substance floats help you identify the substance? Why does one substance float over another?

Write a **Hypothesis:**
Possible hypothesis: Lower density substances float on substances with higher densities. The density of an unknown substance can be approximated by conducting a float test with substances of known densities.

Identify substances by how they float on top of each other.

Materials
- 100-mL graduated cylinder
- blue food coloring
- small piece of cork
- balance and masses
- spoon
- small lump of clay
- small (birthday) candle
- goggles
- four 10-mL graduated cylinders (for measuring the liquid)
- 20 mL each of corn oil, baby oil, corn syrup, and water, each in a plastic cup

Procedures **Safety** Wear goggles.

1. **Measure** Pour 20 mL of water into the 100-mL graduated cylinder, and add one drop of food coloring. Stir.
2. **Measure** Measure out 20 mL of corn oil into a plastic cup. Slowly pour the corn oil down the spoon into the water. Describe what happens.
The corn oil floats on the water.
3. **Experiment** Continue the process in step 2 by adding 20 mL each of the baby oil and then the corn syrup.
The baby oil should float on the water, and the corn syrup should sink.

Conclude and Apply

1. **Compare and Contrast** What happened to the liquids as you added them to the cylinder?
The liquids formed separate layers in the large cylinder.

2. **Communicate** In what order were the liquids arranged? On a separate piece of paper, draw and label an illustration that shows which liquids appeared on top, in the middle, and on the bottom.
The top layer was baby oil, followed by corn oil, then water, and corn syrup on the bottom.

Going Further: Problem Solving

3. **Predict** How will other objects float or sink in the water—a lump of clay, a birthday candle, a piece of cork? Make a prediction and test your ideas.
The lump of clay will sink in water. The candle and cork will float on water.
4. **Experiment** Why do the liquids stack up as they do? How might using equal amounts of the liquids and a balance help you tell?
The liquids stack up in order of density with the lowest density liquid on top and the highest density liquid on the bottom. The relative densities can be verified by comparing the masses of equal volumes of the liquids. (Density = mass divided by the volume.) Use the balance to measure mass.

Inquiry

Think of your own question related to density. Can a higher density material float on a lower density material?

My Question Is:
Possible question: Will the clay float if I form it into a different shape?

How I Can Test It:
Form the clay into a shape with high surface area. Shape the clay and try to float it on water. Reshape the clay until it does float on the water.

My Results Are:
Possible answer: The clay floated when it was formed into a wide, thin- walled boat.

Name ________________ ALTERNATIVE EXPLORE 1

Thinking About Sinking

Materials
- balance
- paper towels
- large bowl of water
- similar-sized cubes of margarine, chocolate, bouillon, and sugar

Procedures

1. Observe the materials your teacher gives you. Compare the volumes of the cubes.
2. If a balance is available, find the mass of each cube. If you do not have a balance, estimate the mass, and rank the cubes from least mass (1) to most mass (4). Record your data in the table below.

Material	Mass	Behavior in Water
Margarine		
Chocolate		
Bouillon		
Sugar		

3. Place each of the cubes in a bowl of water and record what happens.

Conclude and Apply

1. How did the volumes of the four cubes compare?
They were about the same.
2. Which cube seemed to have the most mass? Which had the least mass?
The chocolate had the most mass. The margarine had the least mass.
3. How does the mass of the objects affect what happens when you place them in water?
For a given volume, an object with more mass will sink in water, while an object with less mass will float in water (sugar and bouillon should dissolve).

Name ________________ READING STUDY GUIDE 1
Page 1

Physical Properties

Fill in the blanks.

How Can You Measure Matter?

1. Any solid, liquid, or gas is matter.
2. The more mass an object has, the harder it is to push or pull.
3. The amount of space taken up by an object is its volume.

What Things Float on Others?

4. The amount of mass in a given amount of space is the density of an object.
5. An object that is floating is less dense than the liquid or gas it is in.

How Else Can You Describe Matter?

6. Properties such as color and odor are physical properties.
7. Physical properties can be observed without changing the identify of the substance.

How Can Heat Help to Describe Matter?

8. A substance that changes from solid to liquid or liquid to gas, changes its state.
9. The temperature at which a substance changes from a solid to a liquid is called the melting point.
10. The temperature at which a substance changes from a liquid to a gas is called the boiling point.
11. The particles of a substance will move faster if heat is added to it.
12. When the particles of a substance move about faster, they spread out, causing the substance to expand.

How Can Things Change and Still Stay the Same?

13. Any change that does not produce new substances is a(n) physical change.

Name ________________ READING STUDY GUIDE 1
Physical Properties Page 2

What Are Solids, Liquids, and Gases Like?

14. Something that has a definite shape and volume is called a(n) solid.
15. Something that has a definite volume and takes the shape of its container is called a(n) liquid.

How Can Substances Be Mixed Together?

16. Any combination of two or more substances in which the substances keep their own properties is a(n) mixture.
17. A mixture made of parts that separate upon standing is a(n) suspension.

What Other Types of Mixtures Are There?

18. A mixture in which one substance dissolves in another so that the properties are the same throughout is a(n) solution.
19. The part of a solution that dissolves a substance is called the solvent.

How Do Things Change Identity?

20. New substances are produced with physical properties different from the starting substances in a(n) chemical change.

What Happens to Mass in Chemical Changes?

21. The total mass of all starting substances equals the total mass of all new substances in a chemical change.

Why Do Things Float?

22. When any object is submerged in a fluid, the fluid exerts buoyant force on the object.

How Can We Use Buoyant Force?

23. If the weight of a submerged object is greater than the buoyant force acting on it, the object will sink.
24. Decreasing your density by taking a deep breath helps you float in water.

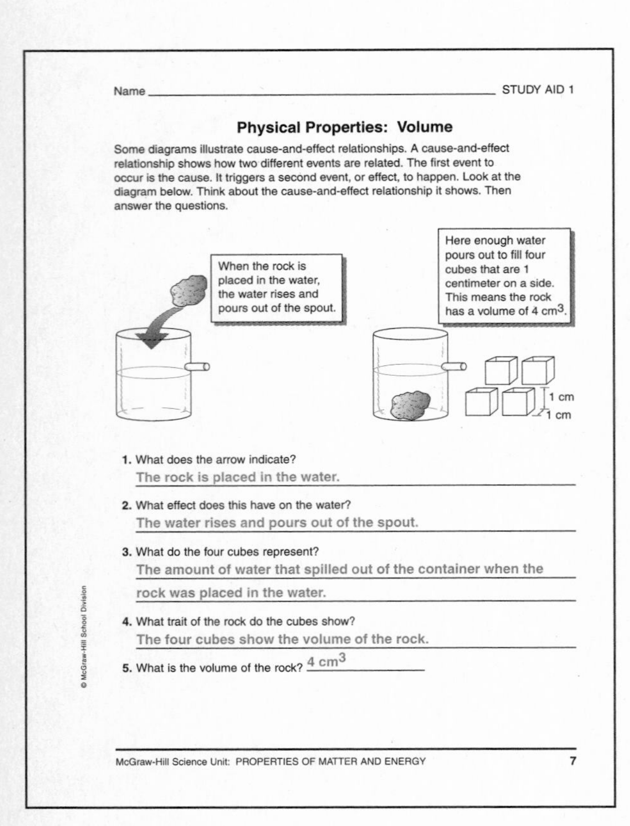

Name ________________ STUDY AID 1

Physical Properties: Volume

Some diagrams illustrate cause-and-effect relationships. A cause-and-effect relationship shows how two different events are related. The first event to occur is the cause. It triggers a second event, or effect, to happen. Look at the diagram below. Think about the cause-and-effect relationship it shows. Then answer the questions.

1. What does the arrow indicate?
   The rock is placed in the water.
2. What effect does this have on the water?
   The water rises and pours out of the spout.
3. What do the four cubes represent?
   The amount of water that spilled out of the container when the rock was placed in the water.
4. What trait of the rock do the cubes show?
   The four cubes show the volume of the rock.
5. What is the volume of the rock? $4\ cm^3$

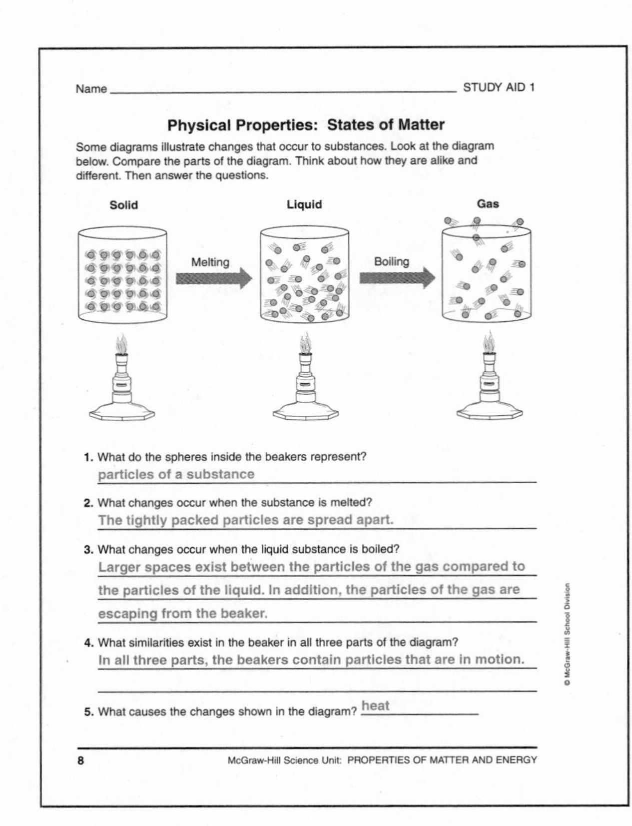

Name ________________ STUDY AID 1

Physical Properties: States of Matter

Some diagrams illustrate changes that occur to substances. Look at the diagram below. Compare the parts of the diagram. Think about how they are alike and different. Then answer the questions.

1. What do the spheres inside the beakers represent?
   particles of a substance
2. What changes occur when the substance is melted?
   The tightly packed particles are spread apart.
3. What changes occur when the liquid substance is boiled?
   Larger spaces exist between the particles of the gas compared to the particles of the liquid. In addition, the particles of the gas are escaping from the beaker.
4. What similarities exist in the beaker in all three parts of the diagram?
   In all three parts, the beakers contain particles that are in motion.
5. What causes the changes shown in the diagram? heat

Name ______ QUICK LAB 1
Page 1

Catch the Gas!

Hypothesize Does total mass change in a chemical change?

Write a **Hypothesis:**
Possible hypothesis: No, the total mass does not change during a chemical reaction.

Materials

- magnesium ribbon
- narrow test tube
- small beaker
- goggles
- vinegar
- balance
- balloon

Procedures

Safety Wear goggles.

1. Half-fill a small test tube with vinegar. Place a thumb's-length piece of magnesium ribbon into the test tube. Stretch the balloon opening over the top of the test tube to form a cap.
2. **Measure** Stand up the test tube in a small beaker. Find the mass of the entire setup. Then observe for a while. Find the mass again. Record your results.
The mass should be the same for both measurements.

Conclude and Apply

1. **Observe** What signs did you observe that a chemical change occurred?
Bubbles formed around the magnesium ribbon. The balloon inflated. The magnesium ribbon got smaller. The vinegar level decreased a very small amount but the change is probably too small to notice.
2. **Compare and Contrast** How did the mass of the starting materials compare to the mass of the materials after the chemical change? Is this what you expected? Explain.
The mass stayed the same. This is to be expected because the system was closed so no mass was lost.

Name ______ QUICK LAB 1
Catch the Gas! Page 2

Going Further How might changing the system affect the measurements of the mass? Write and conduct an experiment.

My Hypothesis Is:
Possible hypothesis: Mass would not be conserved if the system was not closed.

My Experiment Is:
Repeat the experiment without the balloon. Compare the masses before and after the reaction takes place.

My Results Are:
There is a loss of mass. The gas that is produced is given off, so the contents of the test tube decrease in mass. The amount of mass lost is equal to the mass of the gas given off.

Name ______ CLOZE TEST 1

Physical Properties

Fill in the blanks.

In a mixture, two or more substances that keep their own properties are combined. You can use a(n) magnet to separate an iron particle and sulfur mixture. In perfumes, substances are blended together to create pleasing fragrances. However, some of the perfume substances by themselves might have foul odors. Perfume chemists can recognize individual scents. A mixture made of parts that separate upon standing is called a(n) suspension. In this mixture, solid particles separate by settling to the bottom, while fine particles float. Particles can be separated using a(n) filter or strainer. An example of a(n) emulsion is water and oil. These two liquids do not mix together.

Name ______ TOPIC PRACTICE 1

Physical Properties

Match the correct letter with the description.

i 1. any solid, liquid, or gas
b 2. a measure of how hard it is to push or pull an object
d 3. the amount of space taken up by an object
g 4. the amount of mass in a given amount of space
c 5. properties that can be observed without changing the identity of a substance
f 6. the temperature at which a substance changes from a solid to a liquid
j 7. the temperature at which a substance changes from a liquid to a gas
a 8. a combination of two or more substances in which the substances keep their own properties
h 9. a mixture of one substance dissolved in another so that the properties are the same throughout
e 10. a change in matter that produces a new substance with different properties from the original

a. mixture
b. mass
c. physical properties
d. volume
e. chemical change
f. melting point
g. density
h. solution
i. matter
j. boiling point

Answer each question.

11. What happens to an object when it is placed in a less dense liquid or gas?
The object will sink.
12. Name three physical properties that can help identify a substance.
Possible answer: density, melting point, boiling point
13. When swimming, how does taking in a deep breath help you float?
It decreases your density.
14. After a chemical change, which has a greater mass: the starting substances or the new substances?
The masses are equal.

Name ______________________ EXPLORE ACTIVITY 2
Page 1

Design Your Own Experiment

What Is Inside the Mystery Box?

Hypothesize What if you were given a mystery box with things inside? How could you tell what was inside the box without looking inside it?

Write a **Hypothesis:**

Possible hypothesis: In order to determine what is in a mystery box, I would shake the box, tilt the box, and note its relative weight.

Materials

- container, such as a shoe box
- various objects, such as paper clips, marbles, and coins
- paper towels or newspapers (optional)
- ruler
- magnet

Procedures

1. **Plan** (First lab partner) Make a mystery box out of the view of your lab partner. Put various materials in the container. You may line the container with paper towels or newspaper to make it more difficult for your partner to guess what's inside.
2. **Observe/Analyze** (Second lab partner) Observe the shape of the container you are given. Make any measurements you think might help you describe its contents. Note these measurements.
   Students might record the weight and the volume of the box.
3. **Plan** (Second lab partner) Carefully tilt the box. Shake it. Hold the magnet next to the box, and run it back and forth across the surface. Make any observations you can. Write these observations.
   Measurements may range from what the object sounds like, its weight, and its magnetic properties.
4. **Experiment** Switch roles with your partner.

Name ______________________ EXPLORE ACTIVITY 2
Design Your Own Experiment Page 2

Conclude and Apply

1. **Hypothesize** Make a hypothesis about the inside structure or contents of the box. Does it have separate compartments? Record your hypothesis. On a separate piece of paper, draw what you think the inside of the box looks like.
   Answers will vary.
2. **Analyze** How did you develop your hypothesis about the interior structure of the sealed box?
   Students should support their hypothesis with recorded observations.

Going Further: Problem Solving

3. **Hypothesize** What else might you do to try to determine the contents of the sealed box?
   Answers will vary, but may include weighing the box with and without the object.

Inquiry

Think of your own question related to indirect observations. What conclusions do scientists make based on indirect observations?

My Question Is:
Possible question: Can scientists determine the kind of food an animal ate from its skeleton?

How I Can Test It:
Obtain pictures of animal skulls that show the teeth and facial structure. Compare these features in herbivores, carnivores, and omnivores.

My Results Are:
Possible answer: Herbivore: flat teeth, eyes on the side of head, small brain relative to body. Carnivore: sharp, pointed teeth for tearing meat, eyes on front of head, relatively large brain. Omnivores: intermediate characteristics.

Name ______________________ ALTERNATIVE EXPLORE 2

What's Inside?

Materials

- wrapped "mystery present"
- magnet

Procedures

1. Your teacher will give your group an object that is wrapped in paper so that you cannot see what the object is.
2. With your group, discuss some way that you might investigate the object without opening the package and looking inside. List your ideas.
   Students might shake the box or use the magnet to see if the object is hard or magnetic.
3. Use some of the group's ideas to investigate the object. Record the test and the results.

Test	Observation

4. If time permits, exchange "mystery presents" with another group and try to identify the new object.

Conclude and Apply

1. What do you think was in the package? Explain your answer.
   Answers will vary, but the conclusion should be consistent with the observations.
2. Did the group with which you exchanged "mystery presents" come to the same conclusions your group did?
   Answers will vary, but conclusions should be similar.
3. Your teacher will tell you what was in the package. Did you correctly identify the object? If not, what observation do you think misled you?
   Answers will vary.

Name ______________________ READING STUDY GUIDE 2
Page 1

Elements and Atoms

Fill in the blanks.

What Are the Simplest Substances?

1. All matter in the world is made of ___elements___.
2. Elements can be chemically combined to form ___compounds___ like salt and sugar.
3. The smallest particle of an element that has the chemical properties of the element is a(n) ___atom___.

What Is Inside the Mystery Box?

4. For centuries, scientists have been trying to find out what is inside ___matter___.
5. The idea that tiny ___particles___ make up matter came from the Greek philosopher Democritus.
6. John Dalton said that gases were made up of solid particles with ___spaces___ between them.

What Are Atoms Made Of?

7. The densest part of an atom is the ___nucleus___ where most the atom's mass is located.
8. A positively charged particle inside an atom's nucleus is a(n) ___proton___.
9. A particle with no charge inside an atom's nucleus is a(n) ___neutron___.
10. A negatively charged particle that moves around an atom's nucleus is a(n) ___electron___.

How Have Ideas About Atoms Changed?

11. An element's ___atomic number___ is the number of protons in an atom of the element.
12. The mass of an atom is the total number of protons and ___neutrons___.

Name ______________________ READING STUDY GUIDE 2
Elements and Atoms Page 2

What Are Elements Like?

13. Mercury is one of the few elements that is a(n) ___liquid___ at room temperature.
14. While compounds that contain ___calcium___ are common, this substance is never found as an element in nature.

Are There Patterns in the Properties of Elements?

15. The Russian scientist ___Mendeleyev___ discovered a repetitive pattern to several properties of the elements.
16. Mendeleyev's discovery is called the ___periodic table___ of elements.

What Is the Modern Periodic Table Like?

17. In the modern form of the periodic table, elements are arranged in order of increasing ___atomic number___.
18. According to their properties, elements can be placed in one of three groups—___metals___, metalloids, or nonmetals.

What Are Metals and Nonmetals?

19. As a group, metals ___conduct___ electricity.
20. Most nonmetals are poor conductors of ___heat___ and electricity.

What Are Metalloids?

21. The properties of ___metalloids___ fall between the properties of metals and nonmetals.
22. The most abundant element in Earth's solid surface is ___silicon___.
23. Steel is an example of a metallic mixture called a(n) ___alloy___.

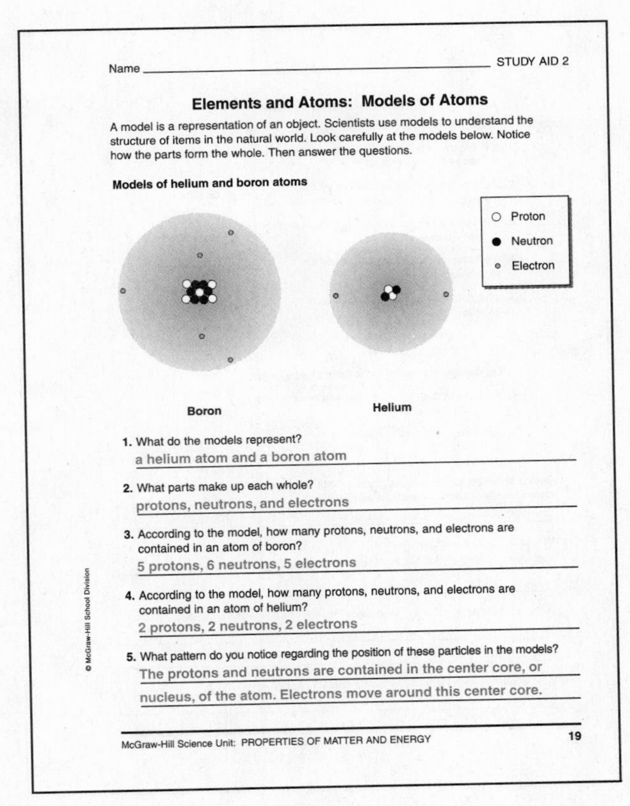

Name ______________________ STUDY AID 2

Elements and Atoms: Models of Atoms

A model is a representation of an object. Scientists use models to understand the structure of items in the natural world. Look carefully at the models below. Notice how the parts form the whole. Then answer the questions.

Models of helium and boron atoms

1. What do the models represent?
a helium atom and a boron atom
2. What parts make up each whole?
protons, neutrons, and electrons
3. According to the model, how many protons, neutrons, and electrons are contained in an atom of boron?
5 protons, 6 neutrons, 5 electrons
4. According to the model, how many protons, neutrons, and electrons are contained in an atom of helium?
2 protons, 2 neutrons, 2 electrons
5. What pattern do you notice regarding the position of these particles in the models?
The protons and neutrons are contained in the center core, or nucleus, of the atom. Electrons move around this center core.

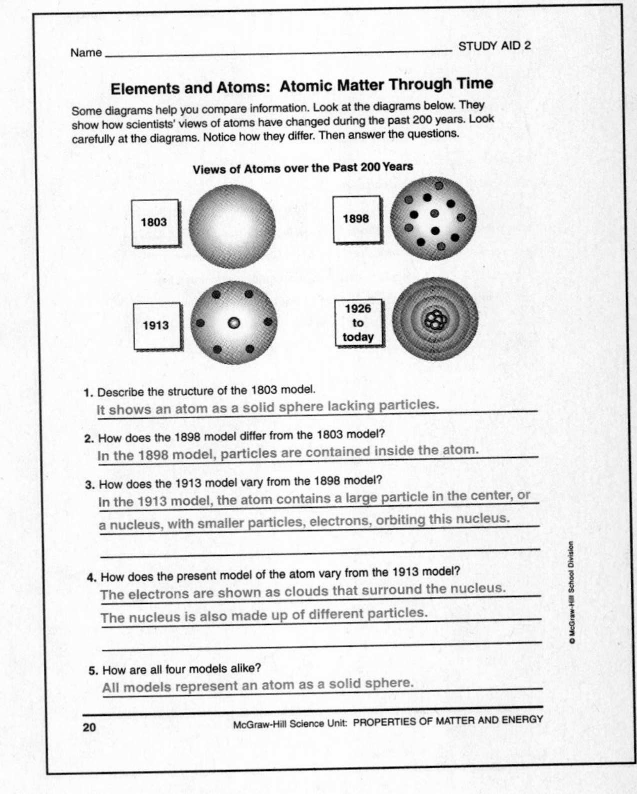

Name ______________________ STUDY AID 2

Elements and Atoms: Atomic Matter Through Time

Some diagrams help you compare information. Look at the diagrams below. They show how scientists' views of atoms have changed during the past 200 years. Look carefully at the diagrams. Notice how they differ. Then answer the questions.

Views of Atoms over the Past 200 Years

1. Describe the structure of the 1803 model.
It shows an atom as a solid sphere lacking particles.
2. How does the 1898 model differ from the 1803 model?
In the 1898 model, particles are contained inside the atom.
3. How does the 1913 model vary from the 1898 model?
In the 1913 model, the atom contains a large particle in the center, or a nucleus, with smaller particles, electrons, orbiting this nucleus.
4. How does the present model of the atom vary from the 1913 model?
The electrons are shown as clouds that surround the nucleus. The nucleus is also made up of different particles.
5. How are all four models alike?
All models represent an atom as a solid sphere.

Name ______ QUICK LAB 2
Page 1

Element Lineup

Hypothesize Some elements are more alike than others. How can you tell which are most alike? Different?

Write a **Hypothesis:**

Possible hypothesis: The similarities and differences among elements can be determined by comparing their structures and properties.

Materials

- element samples (iron, copper, carbon, aluminum)
- sandpaper
- hand lens

Procedures

1. **Plan** All the samples but one belong to a main group of similar elements. Can you tell which belong? Which does not? Decide how you will start. Write your ideas.
   Iron, copper, and aluminum are metals. Carbon is not a metal. Compare physical properties such as color, luster, ductility, and hardness.
2. **Observe** Use the hand lens to look closely at each sample. Note any differences.
   Answers will vary but students should record properties, such as luster and color.
3. **Observe** Rub each sample with sandpaper. What can you learn about each?
   The relative hardness can be determined with the sandpaper. Specific answers may vary due to differences in the form (composition, structure) of the materials selected. Carbon (probably graphite) is likely the softest, followed by copper, then aluminum. Iron is likely the hardest.

Name ______ QUICK LAB 2
Element Lineup Page 2

Conclude and Apply

1. **Analyze** Which characteristics help you identify the most similar samples?
   The three metals where identified by luster, hardness, and ductility.
2. **Analyze** Which sample is most different from the others? How can you tell?
   The carbon sample (graphite) is most different from the others. Graphite is dull, scratches easily, and is brittle. The metals are shiny, more difficult to scratch, and are ductile.

Going Further What other property might you study? Write and conduct an experiment.

My Hypothesis Is:

Possible hypothesis: Metals and nonmetals do not conduct heat equally well.

My Experiment Is:

Press your palm against each material and see which feels warmer or cooler.

My Results Are:

The metals feel cooler. This shows that the metals conduct heat more readily than the nonmetals do. The metals absorb heat from the hand, which is why they feel cool.

Name ______ CLOZE TEST 2

Elements and Atoms

Fill in the blanks.

Metals make up approximately three-fourths of the elements. This group can conduct electricity. Electric wires such as those inside a stereo set or lamp cord are composed of copper. A rubber covering keeps the wires from becoming too hot as electricity travels through them. A poor choice for wires, the metal aluminum would melt if enough electricity went through it. When exposed to water or air, some metals change chemically. Iron rusts when combined with oxygen. Nonmetals usually have properties opposite to metals. At room temperature, most nonmetals are all solids or gases. However, bromine is a(n) liquid at room temperature.

Name ______ TOPIC PRACTICE 2

Elements and Atoms

Match the correct letter with the description.

f 1. a substance that cannot be broken down further into anything simpler
h 2. the smallest particle of an element that has the same chemical properties as the element
d 3. the densest part of an atom where most of its mass is located
b 4. a positively charged particle inside an atom's nucleus
i 5. a particle with no charge located inside an atom's nucleus
e 6. a negatively charged particle that moves around an atom's nucleus
g 7. the number of protons in the atom of an element
a 8. an element that conducts heat and electricity, is shiny, and bendable
c 9. a metallic mixture

a. metal
b. proton
c. alloy
d. nucleus
e. electron
f. element
g. atomic number
h. atom
i. neutron

Answer each question.

10. Before scientists had the correct tools to look inside elements, how did they draw conclusions about the structure of matter?
    They observed physical changes and chemical changes.
11. Why is an atom electrically neutral?
    It is neutral because it has an equal number of protons and electrons.
12. In the modern periodic table, what elements are listed in vertical columns?
    Elements that react with other substances in similar ways are listed in vertical columns.
13. Why would the walls of many buildings contain copper wires?
    The copper wires conduct electricity.

Name ______________________ EXPLORE ACTIVITY 3
Page 1

Investigate How Substances Can Change

Hypothesize Pennies are largely copper. Will a penny turn green, as copper buildings and statues sometimes do?

Write a **Hypothesis:**
Pennies turn green when exposed to certain corrosive environments.

See what happens to a penny in the presence of vinegar.

Materials

- penny
- vinegar
- petri dish
- salt
- clear-plastic cup
- modeling clay
- tweezers
- goggles

Procedures

Safety Wear goggles when you work with vinegar.

1. **Experiment** Place a small wad of modeling clay on the bottom of a petri dish. Wedge a penny in it so that the penny is vertical.
2. Add a small amount of vinegar to the petri dish, and cover it with a clear-plastic cup.
3. **Observe** Describe the color of the penny one hour and three hours later. Describe the color the next day.
   One hour later, the penny should have dark blotches; three hours later, it should turn black; and the next day, it should be green.
4. **Experiment** Use the tweezers to transfer the penny to another petri dish. Cover the penny with a vinegar and salt solution. Observe the penny after one hour, three hours, and one day.
   The black material should disappear.

Conclude and Apply

1. **Infer** What kind of change, if any, was observed in step 3? If you saw a change, was it a chemical or physical change? Explain.
   The penny turned black, then green. The change was chemical.

Name ______________________ EXPLORE ACTIVITY 3
Investigate How Substances Can Change Page 2

2. **Infer** What kind of change, if any, was observed in step 4? If you saw a change, was it a chemical or physical change? Explain.
   The green copper acetate quickly disappeared in the salt-vinegar solution. The black material disappeared more slowly. After one day the penny was a dull reddish-orange color. The changes were chemical.

Going Further: Problem Solving

3. **Hypothesize** Explain the difference between your observations in steps 3 and 4.
   In step 3, the penny reacted with a gaseous mixture of vinegar vapor, water vapor (the vinegar contains water), and air to form a green substance. In step 4, the green substance formed in step 3 reacted with a solution containing liquid vinegar, water, and dissolved salt. The product(s) of the step four reaction was likely dissolved in the salt-vinegar solution since no gaseous or solid reaction products were visible.
4. **Experiment** Find a way to test your hypothesis. You might try repeating the activity using water or club soda instead of vinegar.
   Immerse a clean penny in vinegar to verify the vapor conclusion. If vinegar or salt-water are used in step 4, the green and black substances will disappear.

Inquiry

Think of your own question related to chemical reactions. What other metals or liquids would you like to test? *Show your plan to your teacher before you try it.*

My Question Is: Possible question: Will copper react with bleach? Will steel wool react with water or vinegar?

How I Can Test It: Place the metal sample in the test liquid and/or expose it to the liquid's vapors. Cover the samples. Observe the metal and solution over time.

My Results Are: Copper reacts with bleach to form light green or white crystals. Steel reacts with water to form rust.

Name ______________________ ALTERNATIVE EXPLORE 3

How Will Liquids Affect a Penny?

Materials

- sheet of blank paper
- water
- 4 new pennies
- salt
- 4 small dishes
- lemon juice

Procedures

1. Divide a sheet of paper into four sections. Label the sections: water, salt water, lemon juice, salt and lemon juice.
2. Place a penny in each of 4 dishes, and place one dish on each of the sections of the paper.
3. Add water to the dish labeled *water.* Add water and salt to the dish labeled *salt water.* Add lemon juice to the dish labeled *lemon juice.* Add lemon juice and salt to the disk labeled *salt and lemon juice.*
4. Observe the dishes. Then set them aside for an hour.
5. After an hour, observe the dishes again. Record your observations.

Dish	Observation
Penny in water	
Penny in salt water	
Penny in lemon juice	
Penny in salt and lemon juice	

Conclude and Apply

1. What did you observe immediately after adding the liquids to the pennies?
   Most students will not observe an immediate change.
2. What did you observe after an hour?
   There were small bubbles around the penny placed in salted lemon juice.
3. Based on your observations, what do you think was happening?
   There was some sort of chemical change happening between the penny and the salty lemon juice.

Name ______________________________ READING STUDY GUIDE 3
Page 1

Chemical Changes

Fill in the blanks.

How Can Substances Change?

1. Chemical changes produce substances that have new and different **properties**.
2. A chemical combination of two or more substances is a(n) **compound**.
3. The properties of a compound are different from the **elements** it is made of.

What Happens to Atoms in Chemical Changes?

4. The electrical attraction between atoms forms **chemical bonds**.
5. The ratio in which atoms are bonded together in a compound is shown by a(n) **chemical formula**.

How Do Atoms Form Chemical Bonds?

6. Atoms share electrons in a(n) **covalent** bond.
7. In water, covalent bonds join two **hydrogen** atoms to one oxygen atom.

How Else Can Chemical Bonds Form?

8. A particle that has unequal numbers of protons and electrons is a(n) **ion**.
9. When a sodium ion and a chloride ion join through a(n) **ionic** bond, the compound sodium chloride is produced.

Are All Compounds Made of Molecules?

10. A group of bonded atoms that acts like a single particle is called a(n) **molecule**.
11. The molecules of any given substance are always **alike**.

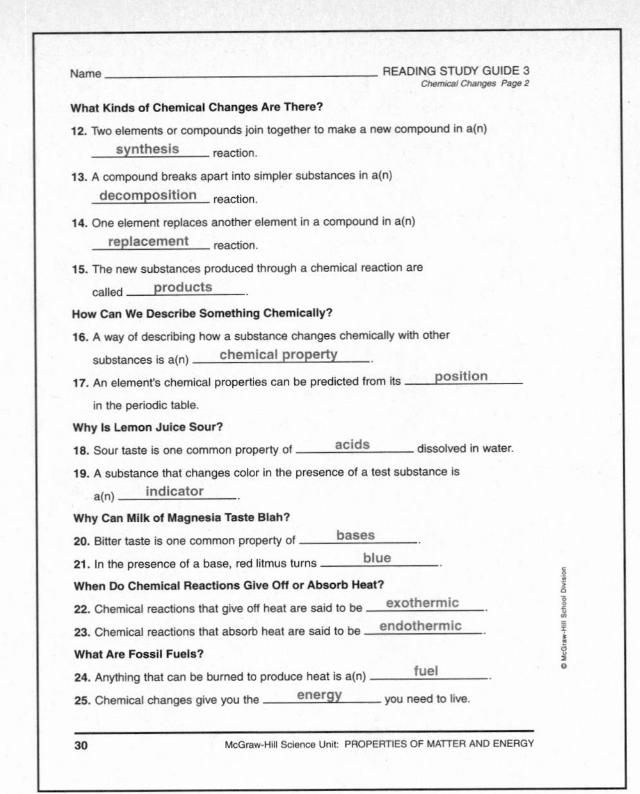
Name ______________________________ READING STUDY GUIDE 3
Chemical Changes Page 2

What Kinds of Chemical Changes Are There?

12. Two elements or compounds join together to make a new compound in a(n) **synthesis** reaction.
13. A compound breaks apart into simpler substances in a(n) **decomposition** reaction.
14. One element replaces another element in a compound in a(n) **replacement** reaction.
15. The new substances produced through a chemical reaction are called **products**.

How Can We Describe Something Chemically?

16. A way of describing how a substance changes chemically with other substances is a(n) **chemical property**.
17. An element's chemical properties can be predicted from its **position** in the periodic table.

Why Is Lemon Juice Sour?

18. Sour taste is one common property of **acids** dissolved in water.
19. A substance that changes color in the presence of a test substance is a(n) **indicator**.

Why Can Milk of Magnesia Taste Blah?

20. Bitter taste is one common property of **bases**.
21. In the presence of a base, red litmus turns **blue**.

When Do Chemical Reactions Give Off or Absorb Heat?

22. Chemical reactions that give off heat are said to be **exothermic**.
23. Chemical reactions that absorb heat are said to be **endothermic**.

What Are Fossil Fuels?

24. Anything that can be burned to produce heat is a(n) **fuel**.
25. Chemical changes give you the **energy** you need to live.

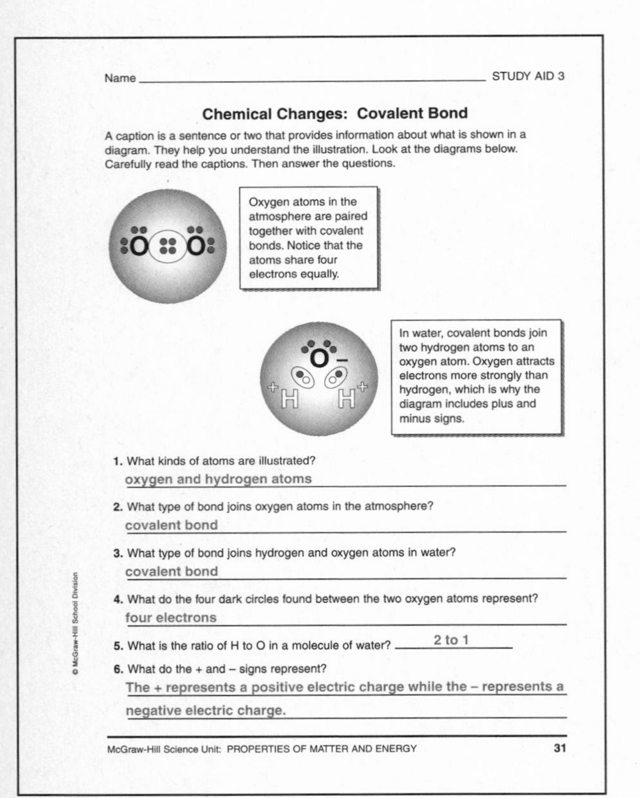
Name ______________________________ STUDY AID 3

Chemical Changes: Covalent Bond

A caption is a sentence or two that provides information about what is shown in a diagram. They help you understand the illustration. Look at the diagrams below. Carefully read the captions. Then answer the questions.

Oxygen atoms in the atmosphere are paired together with covalent bonds. Notice that the atoms share four electrons equally.

In water, covalent bonds join two hydrogen atoms to an oxygen atom. Oxygen attracts electrons more strongly than hydrogen, which is why the diagram includes plus and minus signs.

1. What kinds of atoms are illustrated?
   oxygen and hydrogen atoms
2. What type of bond joins oxygen atoms in the atmosphere?
   covalent bond
3. What type of bond joins hydrogen and oxygen atoms in water?
   covalent bond
4. What do the four dark circles found between the two oxygen atoms represent?
   four electrons
5. What is the ratio of H to O in a molecule of water? **2 to 1**
6. What do the + and – signs represent?
   The + represents a positive electric charge while the – represents a negative electric charge.

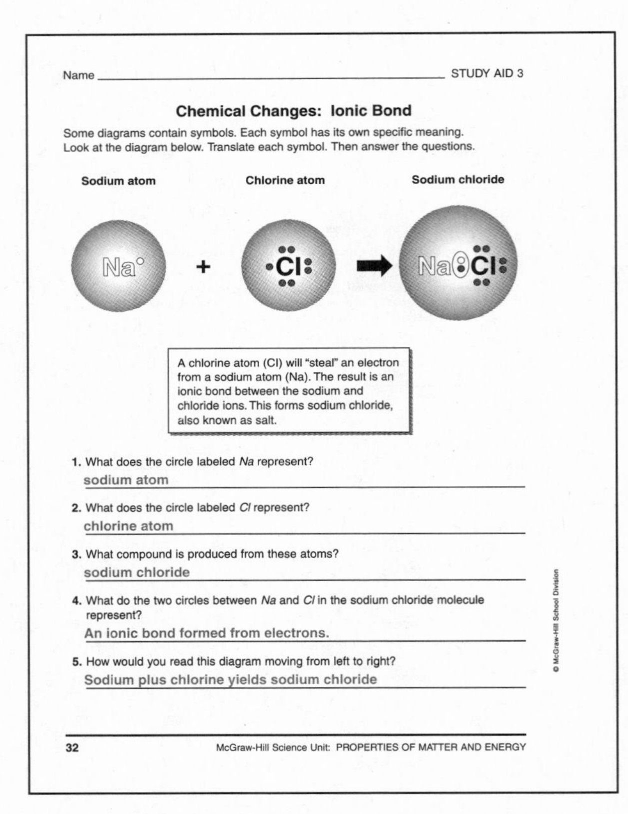
Name ______________________________ STUDY AID 3

Chemical Changes: Ionic Bond

Some diagrams contain symbols. Each symbol has its own specific meaning. Look at the diagram below. Translate each symbol. Then answer the questions.

A chlorine atom (Cl) will "steal" an electron from a sodium atom (Na). The result is an ionic bond between the sodium and chloride ions. This forms sodium chloride, also known as salt.

1. What does the circle labeled *Na* represent?
   sodium atom
2. What does the circle labeled *Cl* represent?
   chlorine atom
3. What compound is produced from these atoms?
   sodium chloride
4. What do the two circles between *Na* and *Cl* in the sodium chloride molecule represent?
   An ionic bond formed from electrons.
5. How would you read this diagram moving from left to right?
   Sodium plus chlorine yields sodium chloride

Name ______________________ SKILL BUILDER 3
Page 1

Using Numbers and Communicating

Chemical Formulas

You can represent almost any substance with a chemical formula. Here are some simple rules for writing formulas. A chemical formula is a simple way to communicate what a compound is made of. Written correctly it can be understood around the world.

1. The elements with the strongest attraction for extra electrons are written last. Elements that are higher up and farther to the right in the periodic table tend to attract electrons more strongly.
2. For molecules, subscripts indicate the actual number of atoms in each molecule. For example, the formula H_2O indicates a molecule with two hydrogen atoms and one oxygen atom.
3. For ionic compounds, subscripts indicate the simplest ratio of ions present.

Materials

- clay of different colors
- periodic table

Cadmium chloride	Potassium fluoride	Carbon monoxide
= Cadmium (Cd) = Chlorine (Cl)	= Potassium (K) = Fluorine (F)	= Carbon (C) = Oxygen (O)

Sulfur trioxide	Carbon tetrachloride	Tetrafluoro ethylene
= Sulfur (S) = Oxygen (O)	= Carbon (C) = Chlorine (Cl)	= Carbon (C) = Fluorine (F)

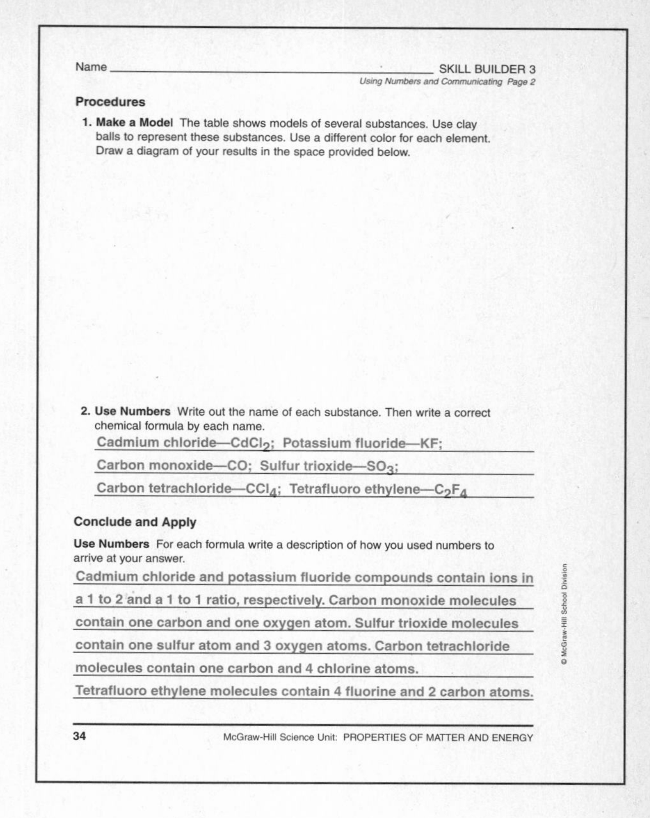
Name ______________________ SKILL BUILDER 3
Using Numbers and Communicating Page 2

Procedures

1. **Make a Model** The table shows models of several substances. Use clay balls to represent these substances. Use a different color for each element. Draw a diagram of your results in the space provided below.

2. **Use Numbers** Write out the name of each substance. Then write a correct chemical formula by each name.
   Cadmium chloride—$CdCl_2$; Potassium fluoride—KF;
   Carbon monoxide—CO; Sulfur trioxide—SO_3;
   Carbon tetrachloride—CCl_4; Tetrafluoro ethylene—C_2F_4

Conclude and Apply

Use Numbers For each formula write a description of how you used numbers to arrive at your answer.
Cadmium chloride and potassium fluoride compounds contain ions in a 1 to 2 and a 1 to 1 ratio, respectively. Carbon monoxide molecules contain one carbon and one oxygen atom. Sulfur trioxide molecules contain one sulfur atom and 3 oxygen atoms. Carbon tetrachloride molecules contain one carbon and 4 chlorine atoms. Tetrafluoro ethylene molecules contain 4 fluorine and 2 carbon atoms.

Name ______________________ CLOZE TEST 3

Chemical Changes

Fill in the blanks.

The original substances in a chemical reaction are called reactants. The products are the new substances produced by the chemical change. Bubbles in soda appear during a(n) decomposition reaction. An example of a(n) synthesis reaction is the rusting of steel wool. During a replacement reaction, one element replaces another in a(n) compound. Elements' chemical properties can be predicted from their periodic table positions. Elements in the first column react immediately on contact with water. Elements in the last column, called the noble gases, rarely form compounds with other elements. Metals in the middle column are more stable than sodium. For this reason, these elements are used to produce coins.

Name ______________________ TOPIC PRACTICE 3

Chemical Changes

Match the correct letter with the description.

d	1. a chemical combination of two or more elements	a. chemical bonds
a	2. the links that atoms or atomic-sized particles can form with one another	b. endothermic
f	3. a way of using letters and numbers to show how much of each element is in a substance	c. molecule
i	4. an electrically charged particle with unequal numbers of protons and electrons	d. compound
c	5. a group of bonded atoms that acts like a single particle	e. fuel
h	6. a way of describing a substance by how it changes chemically with other substances	f. chemical formula
g	7. chemical reactions that give off heat	g. exothermic
b	8. chemical reactions that absorb energy	h. chemical property
e	9. anything that can be burned to produce heat	i. ion

Answer each question.

10. Why does carbon dioxide have the chemical formula CO_2?
    Carbon dioxide contains two oxygen atoms for every one carbon atom.
11. What kind of bonds do nonmetals usually form?
    They usually form covalent bonds.
12. What kind of bond occurs when an atom of sodium joins an atom of chlorine to form sodium chloride?
    It is an ionic bond.
13. What kind of change occurs when iron rusts?
    It is a chemical change.

Name ______________________ CHAPTER PRACTICE
Page 1

Properties and Changes

Circle the letter of the best answer.

1. Any solid, liquid, or gas is
   - a. an ion.
   - (b.) matter.
   - c. solutions.
   - d. weight.

2. The measure of how hard it is to push or pull an object is its
   - a. chemical property.
   - b. density.
   - (c.) mass.
   - d. volume.

3. To calculate the density of an object, you must know the object's
   - a. length and width.
   - (b.) mass and volume.
   - c. physical and chemical properties.
   - d. volume and weight.

4. If an object is placed in a less dense liquid or gas, the object will
   - a. expand.
   - b. float.
   - c. shrink.
   - (d.) sink.

5. Melting point and boiling point are examples of
   - a. chemical changes.
   - b. chemical properties.
   - (c.) physical properties.
   - d. states of matter.

6. A substance that has a definite shape and volume is classified as a(n)
   - a. gas.
   - b. ion.
   - c. liquid.
   - (d.) solid.

7. A color change, heat, and light are signs of a
   - (a.) chemical change.
   - b. mixture.
   - c. physical change.
   - d. solution.

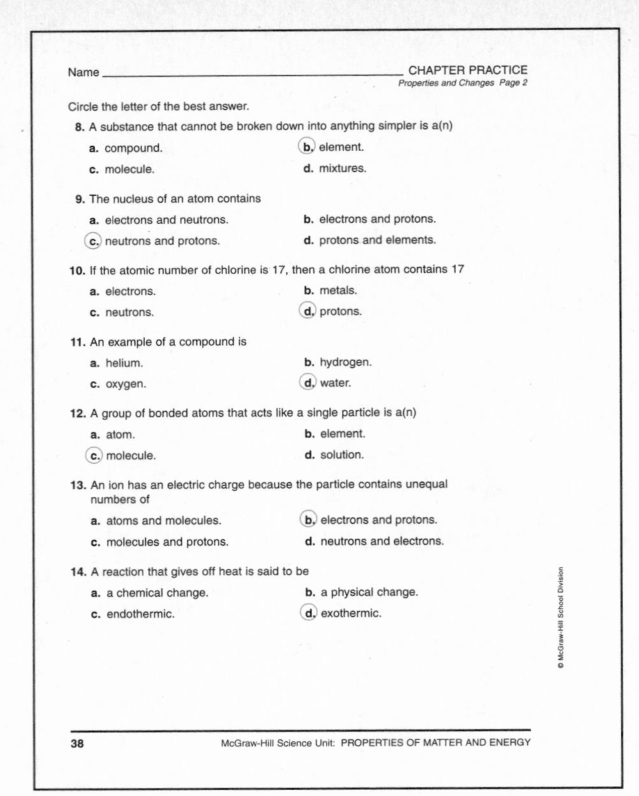

Name ______________________ CHAPTER PRACTICE
Properties and Changes Page 2

Circle the letter of the best answer.

8. A substance that cannot be broken down into anything simpler is a(n)
   - a. compound.
   - (b.) element.
   - c. molecule.
   - d. mixtures.

9. The nucleus of an atom contains
   - a. electrons and neutrons.
   - b. electrons and protons.
   - (c.) neutrons and protons.
   - d. protons and elements.

10. If the atomic number of chlorine is 17, then a chlorine atom contains 17
    - a. electrons.
    - b. metals.
    - c. neutrons.
    - (d.) protons.

11. An example of a compound is
    - a. helium.
    - b. hydrogen.
    - c. oxygen.
    - (d.) water.

12. A group of bonded atoms that acts like a single particle is a(n)
    - a. atom.
    - b. element.
    - (c.) molecule.
    - d. solution.

13. An ion has an electric charge because the particle contains unequal numbers of
    - a. atoms and molecules.
    - (b.) electrons and protons.
    - c. molecules and protons.
    - d. neutrons and electrons.

14. A reaction that gives off heat is said to be
    - a. a chemical change.
    - b. a physical change.
    - c. endothermic.
    - (d.) exothermic.

Name ______________________ EXPLORE ACTIVITY 4
Page 1

Investigate How You Can Tell Warm from Cold

Hypothesize Is your skin a good tool for measuring warm and cool? Can anything affect the way your skin senses warmth?

Write a **Hypothesis:**
Possible hypothesis: Temperature can not be reliably determined by touch. Two different materials that are at the same temperature may not feel equally warm. A material that quickly absorbs heat from your hand feels cool compared to a material that slowly absorbs heat from your hand.

Test how reliable your sense of touch is in telling temperature.

Materials

- 3 cups or glasses

Procedures

1. Fill glass 1 with warm water, not hot water. Caution: Hot water can burn the skin.
2. Fill glass 2 with room-temperature water.
3. Fill glass 3 with cold water from a refrigerator.
4. **Observe** Hold the three middle fingers of your left hand in the warm water. Hold the three middle fingers of your right hand in the cold water. Record the difference in what you feel.
   Possible answer: The left hand feels warm and the right hand feels cool.
5. **Experiment** Hold your fingers in the same glasses again, as in step 4. Then quickly put both the left and right hand fingers in the room-temperature water. What do you feel in each set of fingers?
   Possible answer: The left hand feels cool and the right hand feels warm.

Name ______________________ EXPLORE ACTIVITY 4
Investigate How You Can Tell Warm from Cold Page 2

Conclude and Apply

1. **Hypothesize** When you put both hands in the room-temperature water, did they feel the same? Explain why you felt what you did.
   The right hand felt cool in the room-temperature water because the hand, being warmer, lost heat to the room-temperature water, while heat had previously transferred from the warm water to the hand. The left hand lost heat to both the cold water and the room-temperature water. However, since there was a larger temperature difference between the hand and cold water than the hand and the room–temperature water, the rate of heat loss was less in the room-temperature water, so it felt warmer.
2. **Evaluate** Based on your observations, do you think your skin is a reliable way to tell how hot or cold something is?
   Possible answer: No, the skin is not a good judge of temperature.

Going Further: Problem Solving

3. **Experiment** Try other ways to repeat this activity to investigate your ideas. For example, you might replace the room-temperature water with warm water—or cool water. Safety is important—use warm, never hot, water.
   Answers will vary. Students can try to guess the temperature of the water and check their guesses with a thermometer.

Inquiry

Think of your own question related to temperature. Is your sense of touch unreliable in determining the relative warmth of materials other than water?

My Question Is: Possible question: Do classroom objects seem to be the same temperature when touched?

How I Can Test It: Touch classroom objects that are made from different materials. Record the relative warmth of the objects.

My Results Are: Some room-temperature objects feel cooler than others do. For example, metal objects feel cooler than objects made of wood.

Name ____________ ALTERNATIVE EXPLORE 4

Comparing Hot and Cold

Materials

- different types of cloth
- objects made of metal
- paper
- objects made of wood

Procedures

1. Your teacher will give you a variety of objects.
2. Touch each object and decide if it feels warm or cold to the touch. Record your observations.

Warm Objects	Cold Objects

3. Discuss your results with your group. Check to see if there were objects on which group members disagreed.
4. As a class, discuss your results. Make a list of class results.

Conclude and Apply

1. What kinds of objects seemed warm to the touch?
Most students will likely say that cloth and paper were warm to the touch. Some may also say that wooden objects were warm to the touch.
2. What kinds of objects seemed cold to the touch?
Most students will likely say that the objects made of metal felt cold.
3. Do you think the objects really were at different temperatures? Explain your answer.
Answers will vary, but students should recognize that the objects were all in the same room, so they would all be at room-temperature.

Name ____________ READING STUDY GUIDE 4
Page 1

Temperature and Heat

Fill in the blanks.

How Can You Tell Warm from Cold?

1. The words *hot* and *cold* are used to describe the temperature of something.
2. Any moving object has energy due to its motion.

What Are Two Main Kinds of Energy?

3. The energy of any moving object is called kinetic energy.
4. Energy stored in an object or material is potential energy.
5. The amount of energy needed to raise the temperature of 1 gram of water by 1 degree Celsius is one calorie.

So Just What Is Temperature?

6. The average kinetic energy of the molecules in a material is its temperature.
7. An instrument used to measure temperature is a(n) thermometer.

Does Energy Flow?

8. Before energy can flow between two objects, there must be a difference in the temperatures of the objects.
9. Energy always flows from a hotter object to a(n) cooler one.
10. Energy that flows between two objects because they have different temperatures is called heat.

How Can Heat Move?

11. The transfer of energy by electromagnetic waves is radiation.
12. Objects that absorb electromagnetic radiation receive energy.

Name ____________ READING STUDY GUIDE 4
Temperature and Heat Page 2

What Are Other Ways Heat Can Move?

13. The movement of energy through direct contact is conduction.
14. The transfer of heat by the flow of a liquid or a gas is convection.

Do Some Materials Warm Faster than Others?

15. Equal masses of different materials have a different temperature change for the same amount of heat absorbed.
16. The particular rate at which a material warms up upon absorbing heat is a(n) physical property that can be used to identify a substance.
17. One gram of liquid water rises less in temperature than 1 gram of many other substances per calorie of heat absorbed.

How Can We Keep Heat from Going In or Out?

18. Preventing heat from flowing in or out of a material is called insulation.
19. When you insulate something, you wrap it with a material that is not a good conductor of heat.
20. Since air is a poor conductor of heat, it adds to the insulating ability of fiberglass.

How Do Insulated Bottles Work?

21. Liquids in an insulated bottle stay at their original temperature because heat neither enters nor leaves easily.
22. Microwave ovens use transfer of heat by radiation to cook foods.

Name ______________________________ STUDY AID 4

Temperature and Heat: From Hot to Cold

Sometimes diagrams are used to illustrate changes over time. Such diagrams are usually labeled to show how much time has passed. Look at the diagrams below. Read all labels. Then answer the questions.

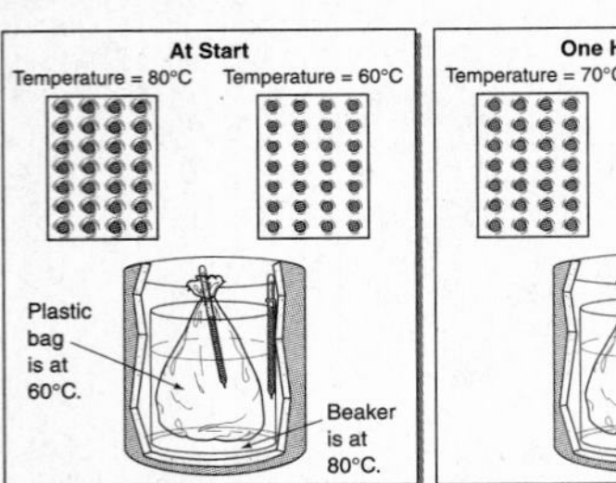

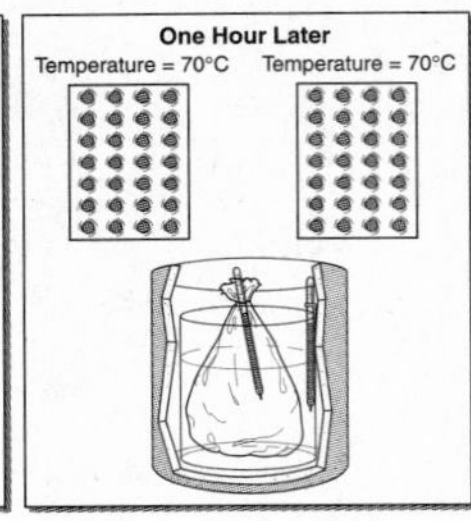

1. How much time has passed between the first and second diagrams? one hour
2. Compare the particles in the first diagram ("At Start").
   The particles in the 80°C beaker vibrates more than the particles in the 60°C bag.
3. Compare the particles in the second diagram ("One Hour Later").
   The particles vibrate an equal amount because they are at the same temperature.
4. What change do the diagrams show?
   They show that the temperature differences of the water were eliminated after a period of one hour.
5. What might have caused this change?
   Transfer of heat energy from the hotter water to the cooler water.

Name ______________________________ STUDY AID 4

Temperature and Heat: Transferring Heat

Different diagrams placed next to each other on a page are usually related in some way. Look at the two diagrams below. Note what each one represents. Think about how they are related. Then answer the questions.

Sauce gets warmer in a pan through the form of heat transfer called conduction.

Cooler air moves in behind the rising warm air. This process is called convection.

Warmer air rises.

Cooler sea breeze

1. Describe what appears to be happening in the pan.
   Heat is flowing from the stove, to the pan, and to the sauce, causing the temperature of the sauce to rise.
2. What is this process called? conduction
3. Describe what appears to be happening to the air over the land.
   The warm land heats the air above it, causing it to rise.
4. What do the arrows represent? motion of the air
5. What is this process called? convection
6. How are these two diagrams related?
   Both diagrams illustrate a process of heat transfer.

Name ______________________________ SKILL BUILDER 4
Page 1

Separating and Controlling Variables

Which Warms Faster—Water or Sand?

Perhaps you have visited a sandy beach on a sunny day and noticed that the sand is too hot to walk on, while the water feels comfortable. Does sand warm up faster than water for the same amount of heat? Design an experiment to answer this question.

In an experiment a variable is something that can affect the outcome. For example, in testing how rapidly water and sand warm up, the length of time the materials are heated would affect their temperature. To make the test "fair", you would have to heat both materials for the same length of time. Making sure that a variable is the same for all samples being tested is called *controlling the variable.*

Materials

- desk lamp
- thermometers
- sand
- water
- 2 containers

Procedures

1. **Hypothesize** Which warms up faster—water or sand? Write a hypothesis.
   Possible hypothesis: Sand heats up faster because 1g of sand experiences a greater temperature change by absorbing 1 calorie of heat than 1g of water.
2. **Use Variables** Make a list of the variables that could affect how rapidly sand and water warm up when heated.
   Variables: amount of each substance, amount of heat applied to each substance, length of time heat is applied, type of containers

Name ______________________________ SKILL BUILDER 4
Separating and Controlling Variables Page 2

3. **Plan** Write a procedure to compare how fast water and sand warm up for the same amount of heat. Have your teacher check your plan.
   Possible answer: 1. Put equal masses of sand and water into identical containers. 2. Place a thermometer in each sample. 3. Check to see that both samples are at room temperature. 4. Record the initial temperature for each sample. 5. Position the containers under the desk lamp so both samples receive equal amounts of heat. 5. Let the samples heat for three hours. 6. Record the temperature of each sample every fifteen minutes.
4. If possible carry out your procedure. Write a report that describes your results on a separate piece of paper. Final temperatures will vary. The sand should heat up more quickly than the water.

Conclude and Apply

1. **Communicate** Summarize your results. Use graphs to show temperature changes of the two substances over time.

Temperature (°C)

Time (hours)

2. Explain your results.
   One calorie of heat will raise the temperature of 1g of sand more than for 1g of water.

Name ______ CLOZE TEST 4

Temperature and Heat

Fill in the blanks.

The transfer of energy by electromagnetic waves is called radiation. These waves can travel through space from the Sun to Earth. On Earth, radiation includes visible, ultraviolet, and infrared waves. Our eyes cannot see infrared radiation. Objects give off visible light when they are heated to 600°C. As the temperature rises to thousands of degrees, the light becomes blue-white. When objects absorb electromagnetic energy, they might change from one state of matter to another, such as snow melting in sunshine. Heat can travel through solids by conduction. It can travel through liquids and gases by another heat transfer called convection. For example, in the atmosphere, warm air rises upward.

Name ______ TOPIC PRACTICE 4

Temperature and Heat

Match the correct letter with the description.

c 1. the energy of a moving object
h 2. energy stored in an object or material
e 3. the average kinetic energy of the molecules in a material
g 4. an instrument that measures temperature
a 5. energy that flows between objects that have different temperatures
d 6. the movement of energy through direct contact
b 7. the transfer of energy by the flow of a liquid or a gas
i 8. preventing heat from flowing in or out of a material
f 9. the transfer of energy by electromagnetic waves

a. heat
b. convection
c. kinetic energy
d. conduction
e. temperature
f. radiation
g. thermometer
h. potential energy
i. insulation

Answer each question.

10. Describe how energy flows between hotter and cooler objects.
Energy flows from hotter objects toward cooler objects.

11. What is the only way heat can travel through solids?
Conduction is the only way heat can travel through solids.

12. Why would air add to the insulating ability of fiberglass?
Air is a poor conductor of heat.

13. Give one example of radiation.
Possible answer: the Sun producing light.

14. Does the same temperature change take place when equal masses of different materials absorb heat?
No, different materials have different temperature changes.

Name ______ EXPLORE ACTIVITY 5
Page 1

Investigate What Heat Can Do to Matter

Hypothesize How does heat affect a gas? How might it affect matter in general?

Write a **Hypothesis:**
Possible hypothesis: Gases expand when heated. In general, matter expands when heated.

See how the size of a balloon is affected by hot and cold.

Materials

- 2 identical balloons
- pan of ice water
- pan of warm water
- modeling compound or clay (optional)

Procedures

1. Blow up the balloons so that both are the same size. Tie each balloon so that no air escapes.
2. **Use Variables** Put one balloon aside, away from either pan of water.
3. **Experiment** Put the second balloon into the warm water for five minutes.
4. **Compare** Remove the balloon from the water. Compare its size with the size of the first. Record your observations.
The balloon that was submerged in warm water is larger than the other balloon.
5. **Experiment** Place the second balloon in the ice water for five minutes. Repeat step 4.
The balloon that was submerged in the ice water is smaller than the other balloon.

Conclude and Apply

1. **Explain** Why did you put the first balloon aside?
The first balloon served as a control sample for comparison.
2. **Communicate** What happened when you put the balloon in warm water? In ice water?
The balloon expanded when placed in warm water and shrank when placed in ice water.

Name ______ EXPLORE ACTIVITY 5
Investigate What Heat Can Do to Matter Page 2

3. **Draw Conclusions** How does heat affect a gas?
A gas expands when it is heated and contracts when it is cooled.

Going Further: Problem Solving

4. **Hypothesize** How might your results change if you used two equal cubes of modeling compound or clay instead of the balloons? How would one cube compare to the other if one was heated in warm water? Cooled in ice water? Write a hypothesis. Test your ideas.
Possible hypothesis: The expansion and contraction would be too small to measure. The clay placed in warm water would soften (become more ductile) and the clay placed in ice water would become firmer.

Inquiry

Think of your own question related to heat and matter. Test the effect of heat or cold on a material of your choice.

My Question Is:
Possible question: How does a rubber ball respond to cold temperatures?

How I Can Test It:
Hold a meterstick vertically, resting it on the floor. Drop a small rubber ball from the top of the meterstick and record how high it bounces. Repeat the bounce measurement 3 times. Place the ball in ice water for 15 minutes. Repeat the bounce test 3 times with the cold ball.

My Results Are:
The cold ball is stiff and does not bounce as high as the room-temperature ball.

Name ______________________ ALTERNATIVE EXPLORE 5

Heating Air

Materials

- hot plate
- pan of water
- heat-resistant bottle with narrow mouth
- balloon

Procedures

Safety Be careful when handling the hot plate.

1. Place a pan of water on a hot plate.
2. Stretch a balloon to make it easier to inflate. Put the balloon on the neck of the bottle. Make sure the balloon is securely stretched over the top of the bottle.
3. Place the bottle in the pan of water. Turn on the hot plate and slowly heat the water. *Caution: Do not heat the water all the way to the boiling point.* Observe what happens to the balloon.
4. Turn off the hot plate and allow the water to cool. Observe what happens to the balloon as the water cools.

Conclude and Apply

1. What did you observe as the water was heated?
   The balloon inflated slightly.
2. What did you observe as the water cooled?
   The balloon deflated.
3. Based on your observations, what generalization can you make about the effect of heat on a gas?
   Answers will vary, but students should recognize that heat makes a gas expand and cold (loss of heat) makes a gas contract.

Name ______________________ READING STUDY GUIDE 5
Page 1

Temperature, Heat, and Matter

Fill in the blanks.

What Can Heat Do to Matter?

1. The expansion of matter when its temperature is raised is called thermal expansion.
2. Before a bimetallic strip turns a thermostat off, heat must cause one side of the metal to expand more than the other side.

What Causes Thermal Expansion?

3. As the temperature of a solid, liquid, or gas is raised, the particles of the substance move faster.
4. Heat causes molecules of a substance to vibrate rapidly which causes the substance to increase in volume.
5. Different materials expand or contract with changing temperature at their own particular rates.

How Do Gas Molecules Push on Surfaces?

6. The force on each unit of area of a surface is called pressure.
7. After air is pumped into a bicycle tire, the pressure inside the tire becomes greater.

What Happens When a Gas Gets Hot?

8. As a gas is heated, the speed at which the gas particles travel increases.
9. The volume of a gas increases when its temperature is raised while keeping its pressure constant.

How Can Heat Change Matter?

10. Adding or removing energy causes matter to change from one state to another.
11. The changing of a solid to a liquid is melting.
12. The change of a liquid to a gas is vaporization.

Name ______________________ READING STUDY GUIDE 5
Temperature, Heat, and Matter Page 2

How Can Cooling Change Matter?

13. The change of a gas into a liquid as molecules attract each other is condensation.
14. The change of a liquid into a solid is called freezing.
15. When bubbles of vapor escape from a liquid as a result of heating, boiling occurs.
16. The vaporization of molecules from the surface of a liquid is evaporation.

What Are Two Ways to Heat a Room?

17. In a steam heating system, water first changes state from a liquid to a(n) gas.
18. The stored heat is then released as water condenses from steam into a liquid.
19. Air in a room is heated by conduction when it comes in contact with the hot pipes of the radiator.
20. Forced-air heating systems do not involve a change of state found in steam heating systems.

How Can Gases Drive a Car?

21. Inside a car engine, heat from burning gasoline warms gases produced by the burning to high temperatures.
22. These gases then push on pistons which propel the car.

How Can Gases Keep Food Cold?

23. A refrigerator moves heat from foods and beverages inside to the air outside.
24. Ice absorbs heat by melting.

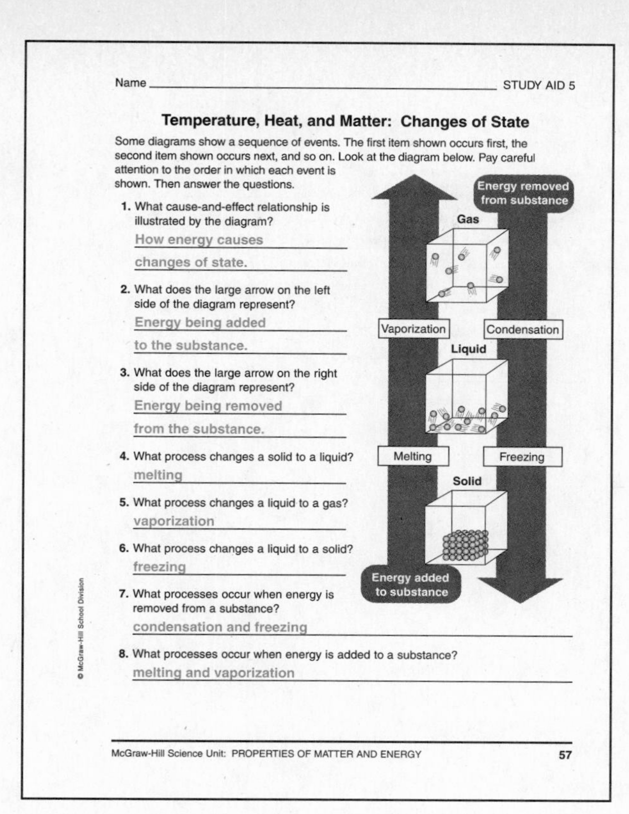
Name ______________________ STUDY AID 5

Temperature, Heat, and Matter: Changes of State

Some diagrams show a sequence of events. The first item shown occurs first, the second item shown occurs next, and so on. Look at the diagram below. Pay careful attention to the order in which each event is shown. Then answer the questions.

1. What cause-and-effect relationship is illustrated by the diagram?
How energy causes changes of state.
2. What does the large arrow on the left side of the diagram represent?
Energy being added to the substance.
3. What does the large arrow on the right side of the diagram represent?
Energy being removed from the substance.
4. What process changes a solid to a liquid?
melting
5. What process changes a liquid to a gas?
vaporization
6. What process changes a liquid to a solid?
freezing
7. What processes occur when energy is removed from a substance?
condensation and freezing
8. What processes occur when energy is added to a substance?
melting and vaporization

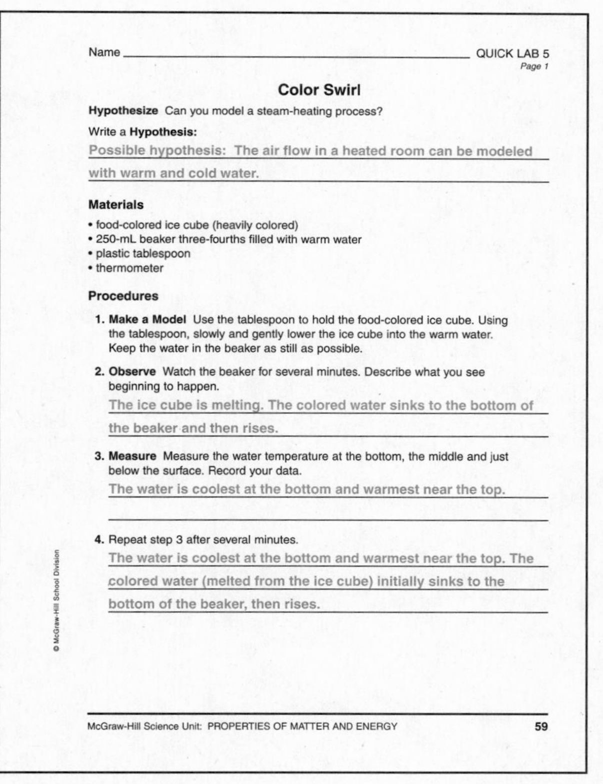
Name ______________________ QUICK LAB 5
Page 1

Color Swirl

Hypothesize Can you model a steam-heating process?

Write a **Hypothesis:**
Possible hypothesis: The air flow in a heated room can be modeled with warm and cold water.

Materials

- food-colored ice cube (heavily colored)
- 250-mL beaker three-fourths filled with warm water
- plastic tablespoon
- thermometer

Procedures

1. **Make a Model** Use the tablespoon to hold the food-colored ice cube. Using the tablespoon, slowly and gently lower the ice cube into the warm water. Keep the water in the beaker as still as possible.
2. **Observe** Watch the beaker for several minutes. Describe what you see beginning to happen.
The ice cube is melting. The colored water sinks to the bottom of the beaker and then rises.
3. **Measure** Measure the water temperature at the bottom, the middle and just below the surface. Record your data.
The water is coolest at the bottom and warmest near the top.
4. Repeat step 3 after several minutes.
The water is coolest at the bottom and warmest near the top. The colored water (melted from the ice cube) initially sinks to the bottom of the beaker, then rises.

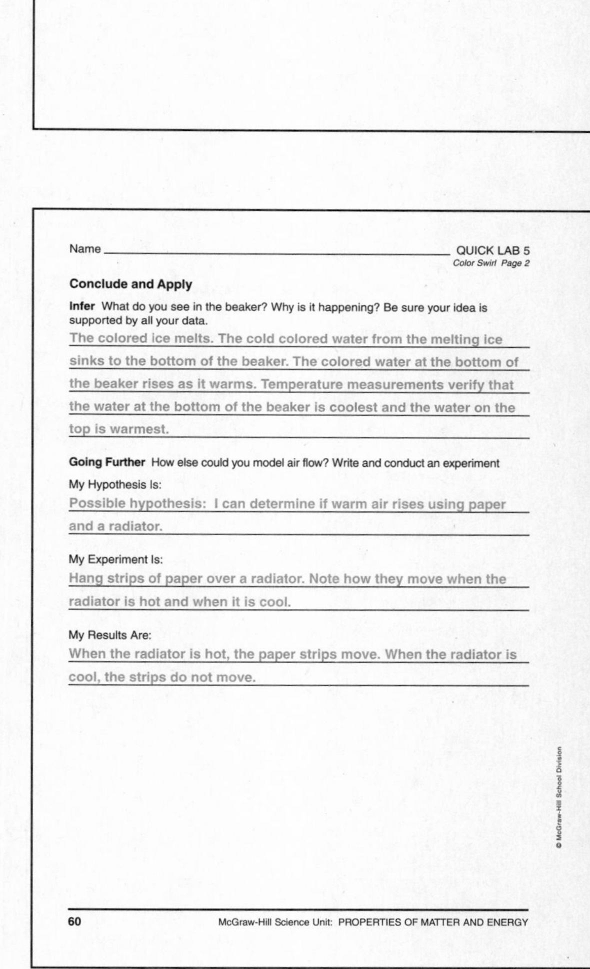
Name ______________________ QUICK LAB 5
Color Swirl Page 2

Conclude and Apply

Infer What do you see in the beaker? Why is it happening? Be sure your idea is supported by all your data.
The colored ice melts. The cold colored water from the melting ice sinks to the bottom of the beaker. The colored water at the bottom of the beaker rises as it warms. Temperature measurements verify that the water at the bottom of the beaker is coolest and the water on the top is warmest.

Going Further How else could you model air flow? Write and conduct an experiment

My Hypothesis Is:
Possible hypothesis: I can determine if warm air rises using paper and a radiator.

My Experiment Is:
Hang strips of paper over a radiator. Note how they move when the radiator is hot and when it is cool.

My Results Are:
When the radiator is hot, the paper strips move. When the radiator is cool, the strips do not move.

Name ______________________ STUDY AID 5

Temperature, Heat, and Matter: Four-Stroke Engine Cycle

Certain diagrams illustrate the steps in a complex process. Look at the diagrams below. They show parts of the four-stroke engine cycle. Read all labels and captions. Then answer the questions.

Intake Stroke

Intake valve
Exhaust valve
Spark plug
Cylinder
Piston
Crankshaft

Low pressure in cylinder pulls in mixture of air and gasoline vapor through open valve.

Piston moves down, causing low pressure in cylinder.

Compression Stroke

Intake valve closes.

Piston moves up and compresses fuel and air.

Power Stroke

Spark plug ignites fuel.

Hot gases expand and push piston down.

Moving piston turns crankshaft, which drives car ahead.

Exhaust Stroke

Exhaust valve opens.

Piston moves up and pushes burned gases out of cylinder.

1. What are the four strokes called?
   intake, compression, power, exhaust
2. During which stroke does the intake valve close? compression stroke
3. During which stroke does the exhaust valve open? exhaust stroke
4. During which stroke are air and gasoline vapor pulled into the engine?
   intake stroke
5. During which stroke does a moving piston turn the crankshaft?
   power stroke
6. What happens immediately after a spark plug ignites fuel?
   Hot gases expand and push the piston down.
7. What causes fuel and air to compress in the engine?
   The piston moves up.

Name ______________________ CLOZE TEST 5

Temperature, Heat, and Matter

Fill in the blanks.

When a solid is heated, particles __vibrate__ rapidly as their temperature rises. Then particles break free from the __forces__ holding them in place. In this process, called __melting__, solids change into liquids. If a liquid is heated, particles will escape and form a(n) __gas__. This transformation of liquid to gas is called __vaporization__. Particles in the gaseous state are spread out because they have freedom of __motion__. As energy is removed from gases, they turn into liquids during __condensation__. Removing energy from liquids cause them to freeze, or turn into __solids__. If liquids are boiled, bubbles of __vapor__ escape. A substance's __temperature__ doesn't change while a change of state occurs.

Name ______________________ TOPIC PRACTICE 5

Temperature, Heat, and Matter

Match the correct letter with the description.

Answer	Description	Choice
d	1. the expansion of matter when its temperature is raised	a. vaporization
e	2. the force on each unit of the area of a surface	b. freezing
f	3. the change of a solid into a liquid	c. evaporation
a	4. the change of a liquid to a gas	d. thermal expansion
h	5. the change of a gas into a liquid	e. pressure
b	6. the change of a liquid into a solid	f. melting
g	7. when bubbles of vapor escape from a liquid as a result of heating	g. boiling
c	8. the vaporization of molecules from the surface of a liquid	h. condensation

Answer each question.

9. What creates the pressure inside a bicycle tire?
   The pressure is created by colliding gas molecules inside the tire.
10. What happens to the volume of a gas when its temperature is raised and its pressure is kept constant?
    The volume of the gas increases.
11. What happens to the temperature of a substance while a change of state occurs? The temperature does not change.
12. What is the main way ice absorbs heat?
    Ice absorbs heat mainly by melting.
13. How is energy transferred in a steam heating system?
    Heat is transferred through changes of state in water.
14. How does a refrigerator keep foods and beverages cool?
    The refrigerator moves heat from the foods and beverages inside it to the air outside.

Name ______________________________ EXPLORE ACTIVITY 6
Page 1

Investigate How to Use Energy from the Sun

Hypothesize How can you use the Sun's energy for useful purposes, such as to cook food?

Write a **Hypothesis:**

Possible hypothesis: The Sun's energy can be used to cook food by using reflective surfaces to focus sunlight onto food.

See how well sunlight can heat food.

Materials

- white construction paper
- unwaxed paper cups
- a peeled apple
- black construction paper
- transparent tape
- aluminum foil

Procedures

1. Place the aluminum foil on top of the white construction paper. The shiny side of the foil should be facing up.
2. Roll the paper and foil into a cone with the bottom narrow enough to fit into the paper cup. Tape the cone so that the cone keeps its shape.
3. Line the inside of one paper cup with black construction paper.
4. Insert the second paper cup into the first. The black construction paper should now be between the two cups.
5. Place small pieces of peeled apple on the bottom of the second cup.
6. Insert the cone, narrow end first, into the second cup and tape it in place.
7. Place the cone in direct sunlight for two hours. Also place small pieces of peeled apple in direct sunlight, next to the cup.

Conclude and Apply

1. **Observe** Look at the pieces of apple every half-hour for two hours. Compare the apple pieces inside the cup and the apple pieces next to the cup.
   Possible answer: The apple pieces inside the cup softened. The apple pieces outside the cup did not soften.

Name ______________________________ EXPLORE ACTIVITY 6
Investigate How to Use Energy from the Sun Page 2

2. **Analyze** What caused the differences you observed? How do you think the cone works?
   The apple pieces inside the cup were heated more than the pieces beside the cup. Sunlight that hits the inside of the cone was reflected down into the cup, concentrating the sunlight and heating the apple.

Going Further: Problem Solving

3. **Plan** Would other food items show the same results? Write a hypothesis. How would you test it?
   A variety of foods can be cooked in a solar oven made from reflective materials. Possible test: Make a box lined with reflective metal (shiny aluminum). Make a lid that can be propped up at different angles. Make a second inner lid from clear plastic or glass. Place a dark piece of metal in the bottom of the box to absorb heat. Insulate the box. Try heating pizza bagels or prepared cookie dough in the oven.

Inquiry

Think of your own question related to solar energy. How hot do solar ovens need to be to cook food?

My Question Is:
Possible question: How much hotter was it inside the cup than outside the cup?

How I Can Test It:
Repeat the steps in the Procedures with a thermometer in the cup and a thermometer beside the cup.

My Results Are:
Answers will vary. A solar oven must be substantially warmer than the air temperature to cook food.

Name ______________________________ ALTERNATIVE EXPLORE 6

Capturing Solar Energy

Materials

- boxes
- glue
- magnifying glass
- timer
- pieces of cardboard
- aluminum foil
- marshmallows
- thermometer
- tape
- scissors
- pencil
- towels

Procedures

1. Work with a group to design a solar cooker. Discuss with your group ways to capture the Sun's energy and concentrate it on an object. Also discuss how you can test the cooker to evaluate your design.
2. Make a sketch of your group's plan below. Show the plan to your teacher before you begin to construct your solar cooker.
3. After you receive approval from your teacher, construct your solar cooker.
4. On a sunny day, take your cooker outdoors and test it.

Conclude and Apply

1. What method did your group decide to use to concentrate the Sun's energy?
   Students will likely use a magnifying glass or a curved reflector.
2. What method did your group agree to use as a test of the cooker?
   Answers will vary. Some groups may place a thermometer in the cooker and measure the temperature increase. Other groups may try to cook something, such as a marshmallow.
3. Was your design successful? If not, how could you modify your design to make it work better?
   Answers will vary. Using a magnifying glass with aluminum foil as a base could improve a design.

Name ______________________ READING STUDY GUIDE 6
Page 1

Sources of Energy

Fill in the blanks.

How Can the Sun's Energy Be Used?

1. Plants convert the Sun's energy into chemical energy stored in compounds called carbohydrates.
2. The Sun's energy heats a fluid as it passes through pipes in a(n) active solar heating system.
3. Heat from the Sun is stored in a thick wall in a(n) passive solar heating system.

How Can Sunlight Be Turned into Electricity?

4. A device that generates an electric current from sunlight is a(n) solar cell.
5. Some power plants use mirrors to focus the Sun's rays onto a collector where water is heated to boiling.

Why Are Fossil Fuels Called Fossil Fuels?

6. Coal, oil, and natural gas give off large amounts of heat when burned.
7. Fossils fuels are examples of nonrenewable resources because they take millions of years to form.

Can Modern Plant and Animal Matter Give Us Energy?

8. Getting energy from plant and animal materials by changing them into high-quality fuels is called biomass conversion.
9. The fuels produced through biomass conversion are renewable resources.

How Can Atomic Nuclei Produce Energy by Splitting?

10. The splitting of a nucleus with a large mass into two nuclei with smaller masses is called nuclear fission.

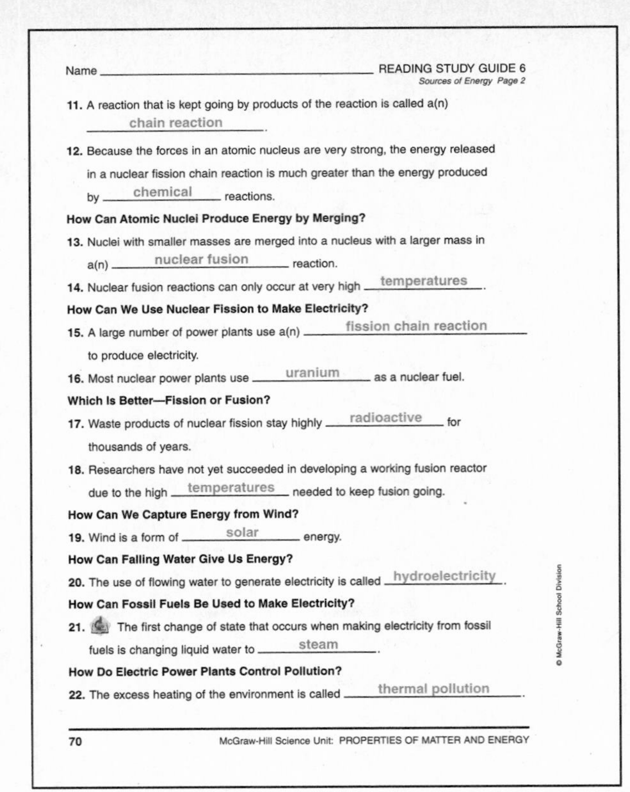
Name ______________________ READING STUDY GUIDE 6
Sources of Energy Page 2

11. A reaction that is kept going by products of the reaction is called a(n) chain reaction.
12. Because the forces in an atomic nucleus are very strong, the energy released in a nuclear fission chain reaction is much greater than the energy produced by chemical reactions.

How Can Atomic Nuclei Produce Energy by Merging?

13. Nuclei with smaller masses are merged into a nucleus with a larger mass in a(n) nuclear fusion reaction.
14. Nuclear fusion reactions can only occur at very high temperatures.

How Can We Use Nuclear Fission to Make Electricity?

15. A large number of power plants use a(n) fission chain reaction to produce electricity.
16. Most nuclear power plants use uranium as a nuclear fuel.

Which Is Better—Fission or Fusion?

17. Waste products of nuclear fission stay highly radioactive for thousands of years.
18. Researchers have not yet succeeded in developing a working fusion reactor due to the high temperatures needed to keep fusion going.

How Can We Capture Energy from Wind?

19. Wind is a form of solar energy.

How Can Falling Water Give Us Energy?

20. The use of flowing water to generate electricity is called hydroelectricity.

How Can Fossil Fuels Be Used to Make Electricity?

21. The first change of state that occurs when making electricity from fossil fuels is changing liquid water to steam.

How Do Electric Power Plants Control Pollution?

22. The excess heating of the environment is called thermal pollution.

© McGraw-Hill School Division

70 McGraw-Hill Science Unit: PROPERTIES OF MATTER AND ENERGY

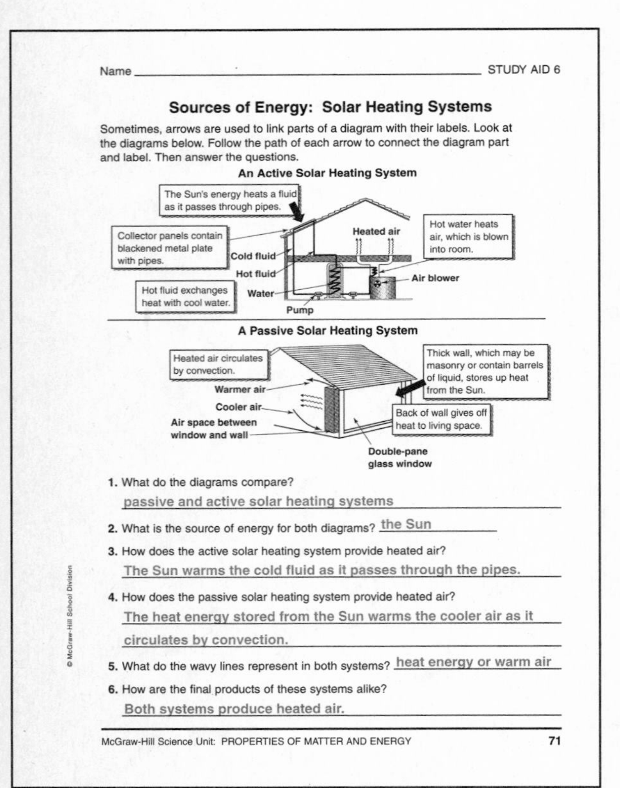
Name ______________________ STUDY AID 6

Sources of Energy: Solar Heating Systems

Sometimes, arrows are used to link parts of a diagram with their labels. Look at the diagrams below. Follow the path of each arrow to connect the diagram part and label. Then answer the questions.

1. What do the diagrams compare? passive and active solar heating systems
2. What is the source of energy for both diagrams? the Sun
3. How does the active solar heating system provide heated air? The Sun warms the cold fluid as it passes through the pipes.
4. How does the passive solar heating system provide heated air? The heat energy stored from the Sun warms the cooler air as it circulates by convection.
5. What do the wavy lines represent in both systems? heat energy or warm air
6. How are the final products of these systems alike? Both systems produce heated air.

© McGraw-Hill School Division

McGraw-Hill Science Unit: PROPERTIES OF MATTER AND ENERGY 71

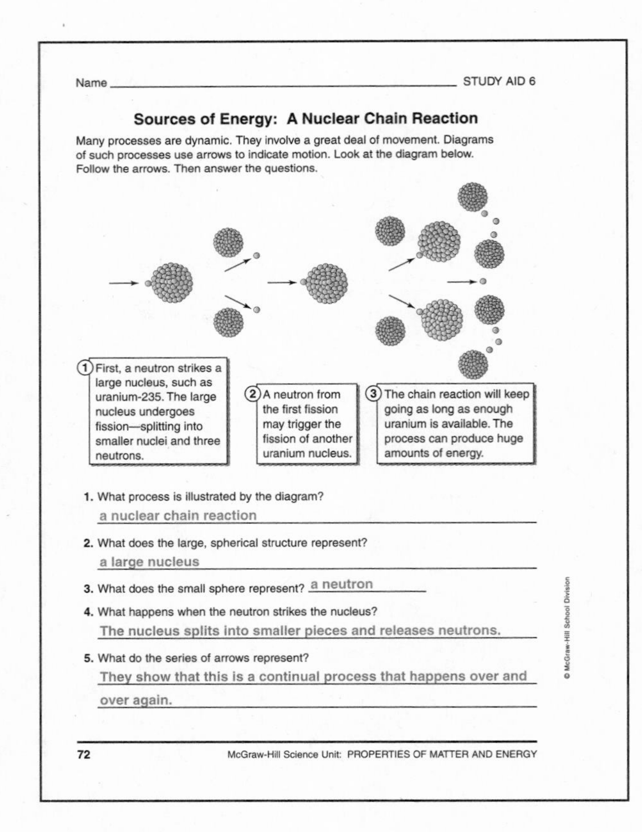
Name ______________________ STUDY AID 6

Sources of Energy: A Nuclear Chain Reaction

Many processes are dynamic. They involve a great deal of movement. Diagrams of such processes use arrows to indicate motion. Look at the diagram below. Follow the arrows. Then answer the questions.

1. What process is illustrated by the diagram? a nuclear chain reaction
2. What does the large, spherical structure represent? a large nucleus
3. What does the small sphere represent? a neutron
4. What happens when the neutron strikes the nucleus? The nucleus splits into smaller pieces and releases neutrons.
5. What do the series of arrows represent? They show that this is a continual process that happens over and over again.

© McGraw-Hill School Division

72 McGraw-Hill Science Unit: PROPERTIES OF MATTER AND ENERGY

Name ____________ QUICK LAB 6
Page 1

A Chain Reaction

Hypothesize How can you use everyday materials to model a nuclear chain reaction?

Write a **Hypothesis:**
Possible hypothesis: Everyday materials, such as clay and beans, can be used to model a chain reaction by demonstrating sequential collisions and the results of these collisions.

Materials

- everyday materials

Procedures

1. **Plan** Decide on everyday materials that you can use. You might choose foam balls, dried beans, or squares of colored paper to model the nuclei and neutrons. You could present your model on a poster, in a diorama, or as an activity involving your classmates. Record your choice of materials and what they will represent.
Students might choose clay and beans to represent protons and neutrons. Form a ball of clay to represent protons in the nucleus. Poke beans into the clay to represent neutrons.
2. **Make a Model** With your teacher's approval, build your model. Your teacher may ask you to write an explanation of the model or to discuss the model with the class.
Possible model: A bean (neutron) is shown colliding with a ball made from clay and beans (nucleus). The ball splits in half and 3 beans separate from the ball. These three beans hit 3 other balls. Each ball splits in two and releases 3 beans.

Name ____________ QUICK LAB 6
A Chain Reaction Page 2

Conclude and Apply

Evaluate In what ways was your model successful? In what ways was it not successful?
Models likely show collisions and resulting separations well, but do not show how energy is released during the chain reaction.

Going Further How else could you model the reaction? Write and conduct an experiment.

My Hypothesis Is:
Possible hypothesis: I can use falling dominoes to show a nuclear reaction.

My Experiment Is:
Set up a line of five or six dominoes. Then put two dominoes side by side to start two parallel lines. Continue setting up a branching pattern. Push over the first domino to see if one change can set off many other changes.

My Results Are:
When one domino falls and hits two dominoes, the motion continues down two lines. This is like a chain reaction, when splitting one atom causes more atoms to split.

Name ____________ CLOZE TEST 6

Sources of Energy

Fill in the blanks.

Wind is a type of solar energy. It is created by the uneven heating of Earth's surface by the Sun. Windmills have been used on farms to pump water and grind grain. Some remote areas also used wind-powered electric generators. The need for these lessened when electric companies strung wires across America. On wind farms, wind is converted into electricity using large wind turbines. The kinetic energy of falling water can be harnessed to turn a wheel. Flowing water is used to generate electricity in a process called hydroelectricity. This method causes little pollution and is readily available. However, building large dams can damage the environment.

Name ____________ TOPIC PRACTICE 6

Sources of Energy

Match the correct letter with the description.

j 1. plants convert the Sun's energy into chemical energy stored in these
f 2. fossil fuels
b 3. how plant and animal materials are changed into high-quality fuels
d 4. the fuels produced from biomass conversion
h 5. the splitting of a nucleus with a large mass into two nuclei with smaller masses
a 6. when nuclei with smaller masses are merged to make a nucleus with a larger mass
e 7. nuclear plants use fission chain reactions to produce this
g 8. the use of flowing water to generate electricity
i 9. the excess heating of the environment
c 10. when products of a reaction keep the reaction going

a. nuclear fusion
b. biomass conversion
c. chain reaction
d. renewable resources
e. electricity
f. nonrenewable resources
g. hydroelectrical energy
h. nuclear fission
i. thermal pollution
j. carbohydrates

Answer each question.

11. What can a solar cell generate from sunlight?
A solar cell can generate an electric current from sunlight.
12. Why are coal, oil, and natural gas good fuels?
They are good fuels because they give off large amounts of heat when burned.
13. What kinds of temperature are required for a nuclear fusion reaction to take place?
Very high temperatures are needed for a nuclear fusion reaction.

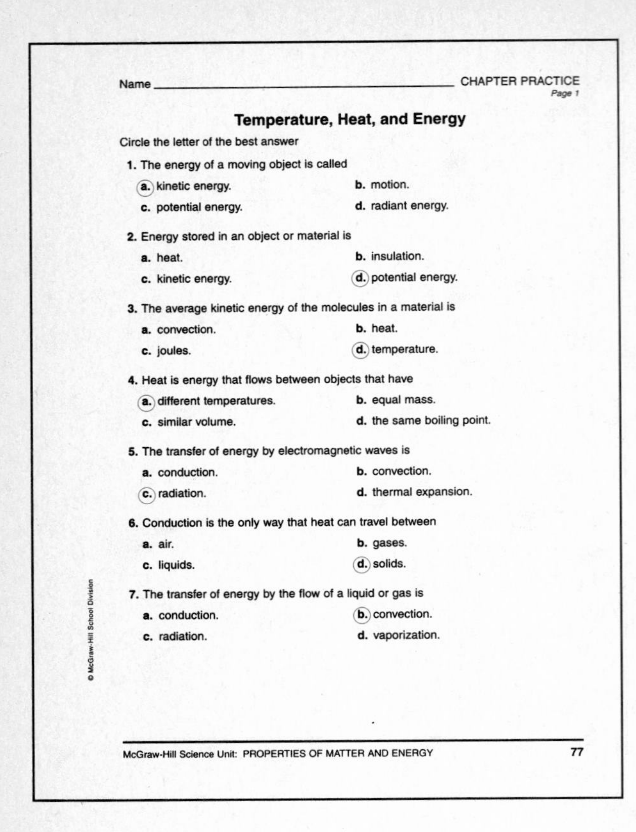

Name ____________________ CHAPTER PRACTICE
Page 1

Temperature, Heat, and Energy

Circle the letter of the best answer

1. The energy of a moving object is called
   a. kinetic energy. b. motion.
   c. potential energy. d. radiant energy.

2. Energy stored in an object or material is
   a. heat. b. insulation.
   c. kinetic energy. d. potential energy.

3. The average kinetic energy of the molecules in a material is
   a. convection. b. heat.
   c. joules. d. temperature.

4. Heat is energy that flows between objects that have
   a. different temperatures. b. equal mass.
   c. similar volume. d. the same boiling point.

5. The transfer of energy by electromagnetic waves is
   a. conduction. b. convection.
   c. radiation. d. thermal expansion.

6. Conduction is the only way that heat can travel between
   a. air. b. gases.
   c. liquids. d. solids.

7. The transfer of energy by the flow of a liquid or gas is
   a. conduction. b. convection.
   c. radiation. d. vaporization.

© McGraw-Hill School Division

McGraw-Hill Science Unit: PROPERTIES OF MATTER AND ENERGY 77

Name ____________________ CHAPTER PRACTICE
Temperature, Heat, and Energy Page 2

Circle the letter of the best answer.

8. Preventing heat from flowing in or out of a material is called
   a. conduction. b. convection.
   c. insulation. d. melting.

9. The vaporization of molecules from the surface of a liquid is
   a. condensation. b. evaporation.
   c. freezing. d. melting.

10. A gas changes into a liquid through
    a. condensation. b. convection.
    c. evaporation. d. vaporization.

11. The splitting of a nucleus with a large mass into two nuclei with smaller masses is called
    a. biomass conversion. b. hydroelectricity.
    c. nuclear fission. d. nuclear fusion.

12. A device that generates electric current from sunlight is a(n)
    a. active solar heating system. b. nuclear reactor.
    c. passive solar heating system. d. solar cell.

13. The merging of nuclei with smaller masses into a nucleus with a larger mass is called
    a. biomass conversion. b. chain reactions.
    c. nuclear fusion. d. thermal pollution.

14. The fuels produced through biomass conversion are
    a. fossil fuels. b. nonrenewable resources.
    c. renewable resources. d. solar cells.

© McGraw-Hill School Division

78 McGraw-Hill Science Unit: PROPERTIES OF MATTER AND ENERGY